Fifty Years of
Children's Books

DORA V. SMITH
Photo by *Minneapolis Sunday Tribune*

Fifty Years of Children's Books
1910-1960: Trends, Backgrounds, Influences

By

DORA V. SMITH

Designed by

NORMA PHILLIPS

ncte *The National Council of Teachers of English*

508 SOUTH SIXTH STREET, CHAMPAIGN, ILLINOIS

NATIONAL COUNCIL OF TEACHERS OF ENGLISH
COMMITTEE ON PUBLICATIONS

James R. Squire, Executive Secretary, NCTE, *Chairman*
Robert A. Bennett, Minneapolis Public Schools
Autrey Nell Wiley, Texas Woman's University
Miriam E. Wilt, Temple University
Enid M. Olson, Director of Publications, NCTE

Preface

Many years of intimate association with children's books, with those who know them best, and with those who understand the power of books to enrich the lives of boys and girls have gone into the making of this book. From college days on, it has been the author's good fortune to share the inspiration of such leaders as Isabel M. McLaughlin and Della McGregor, for many years children's librarians of the Minneapolis and St. Paul Public Libraries, and of Margaret R. Greer, librarian of the Minneapolis Public Schools. Then followed equally rewarding associations with Phyllis Fenner, a librarian in the Manhasset Public Schools in New York, and with Nora Beust, formerly head of the School Libraries Division of the United States Office of Education.

Directors of teaching, too, like Dr. Muriel Crosby, Assistant Superintendent in charge of Elementary Education in Wilmington, Delaware, and recent chairman of the Elementary Book List Committee of the National Council of Teachers of English; May Hill Arbuthnot, formerly of Western Reserve University, who taught the courses in Children's Literature; and Dr. Bernice Leary, recently Curriculum Consultant in the public schools of Madison, Wisconsin, have been a constant source of inspiration together with thousands of teachers and prospective teachers of this country who have proved by their enthusiasm and their desire to know, how rewarding a knowledge of children's books can be. This is the spirit in which *Fifty Years of Children's Books* was written—to open up the field (not to exhaust it), to give some inkling of the rewards in store, and to furnish leads by which the reader may expand his own knowledge of the field.

The privilege of intimate acquaintance with both teachers and librarians has made the author aware of how little they sometimes know of one another. For that reason, the volume emphasizes the contributions of both groups to the development of children's books and suggests how much they could do *together*. Publishers, too, have determined, in large part, the course which children's books have taken, and the writers and illustrators of books have enriched the program for all concerned.

Determination of the "significant" books of fifty years is a subjective task. Significant for what? Perhaps for children, perhaps for the direction which book-making will take next, perhaps for illustration or format, perhaps for style of writing, for validity of facts, for stimulation of the imagination. Each writer on the subject has his own standards. The list given here presents the author's personal evaluation. It can claim to do nothing else. Suggested grade placement follows that of the *Children's Catalog* whenever it is given there.

The bibliographical details of such a study are both elusive and overwhelming.

The writer is indebted to the resources of the University of Minnesota Library and especially to Professor James Kingsley, Jr., chief of special collections, including the Kerlan Collection of children's books, and to the Departments of Bibliography and Reference for patient help and encouragement. Miss Bette J. Peltala of the staff in Children's Literature offered valuable assistance. The Library of Congress and the New York Public Library likewise cooperated.

The American Library Association has also helped greatly. The author is indebted especially to Mildred L. Batchelder, Executive Secretary of its Children's Services Division and its Young Adult Services Division, who encouraged the publication of this book, and to her and her associates, Mrs. Sidney Renthal and Miss Donna Secrist, librarians of the Evanston Public Schools, for bibliographical help. To Marion Kellogg, librarian of the Jackson Intermediate School in Detroit, and to Ruth Ersted, Supervisor of School Libraries in the Minnesota State Department of Education, the author owes both encouragement and information.

To the publishers, thanks are due for their generous gift of illustrations from the books discussed and for their gracious response to inquiries by mail.

Those who read the manuscript and made helpful suggestions for the improvement of it have the sincere gratitude of the author. They include Margaret M. Clark, Head of the Lewis Carroll Room of the Cleveland Public Library; Dr. Muriel Crosby, Assistant Superintendent of Schools in Wilmington, Delaware, and past chairman of the Elementary Book List Committee of the National Council of Teachers of English; Dr. Constance McCullough, Reading Specialist at San Francisco State College; Dr. John J. DeBoer, Professor of Education at the University of Illinois and former editor of *Elementary English;* and members of the Committee on Publications of the National Council of Teachers of English.

The task of editing a book of this nature is an interminable one. The author acknowledges with very special thanks the patient and expert assistance of Mrs. Enid Olson and her associates in the office of the National Council of Teachers of English.

If *Fifty Years of Children's Books* brings happy recollections and a few new facts to those who have enjoyed a lifetime of reading and leads those new to the field to taste its joys, the book will have fulfilled the author's purpose.

Dora V. Smith

Minneapolis, Minnesota
March, 1963

Acknowledgements

The author and publishers wish to thank the following publishers, authors and agents for permission to reprint material published in this book:

DOUBLEDAY & COMPANY, INC., for the quotation from *Fairy Tales Every Child Should Know* by Hamilton Wright Mabie. Published and copyright by Doubleday & Company in 1914.

E. P. DUTTON & CO., INC., for the quotations from *A Child's Day* by Walter de la Mare. Published and copyright by E. P. Dutton & Co. in 1915. Published in the British Commonwealth by CONSTABLE YOUNG BOOKS, LTD. For the same quotations, THE SOCIETY OF AUTHORS. Reprinted by permission of The Literary Trustees of Walter de la Mare and The Society of Authors as their representative.

LITTLE, BROWN AND COMPANY for the quotation from *Old Mother West Wind* by Thornton Burgess, Golden Anniversary Edition. Published and copyright by Little, Brown and Company in 1960.

SATURDAY REVIEW for the quotation from "Noble Boys" by Clarence Day in *Saturday Review*, XV (November 14, 1936). Reprinted with permission of ALFRED A. KNOPF, INC., from *The Best of Clarence Day*. Copyright 1936 by The Estate of Clarence Day.

UNIVERSITY OF CHICAGO PRESS for the quotation from "The Psychological Case Against the Fairy Tale" by H. E. Wheeler in the *Elementary School Journal*, XXIX (June, 1929). Copyright 1929 by The University of Chicago.

Table of Contents

List of Illustrations

Introduction

"Fifty Years of Children's Books," an address by Dora V. Smith, was the highlight of the Books for Children Luncheon of the Golden Anniversary Convention of the National Council of Teachers of English in 1960. More than presenting an interesting and vital subject to teachers and students of children's literature, the occasion was marked by added significance because of the speaker. Through long years of devoted and dynamic leadership, Dora Smith has brought to the Council a love of the English language and an ability to communicate this love to others, the integrity of scholarship and the ability to distinguish between quality and showmanship, and a deep commitment to children and teachers with the skill to interpret this commitment in action.

The participants in the Golden Anniversary Books for Children Luncheon were deeply sensitive to the fact that they were present at a moment when a respected and admired colleague was engaged in a presentation of a distinguished contribution to teaching and learning. It seems only fitting, therefore, that the scholarly research, the sensitive feeling for children and books, the distillation of knowledge and wisdom of one of the Council's truly great leaders should be made available as a publication of the Council in 1963.

A study of *Fifty Years of Children's Books* is more than a reading of historical fact; it is an exhilarating and refreshing experience for the reader. The significance of this volume lies not alone in its value to teachers and scholars in reviewing interesting developments in the creation of a highly specialized body of literature uniquely designed for children. Its greater significance is in the portrayal of children's literature in its setting of fifty years of living and learning—about children and how they grow and learn—about education and its changing function and purpose—about human beings whose concepts and ideals are changing as new knowledge of the universe and man's place in it evolve. If the reader is able to "catch" some of the deeply penetrating insight, the keen sensitivity to the interaction of the forces affecting the lives of people, and the appreciation of what books can mean to children which the author reveals in *Fifty Years of Children's Books,* the rewards will be rich.

In the books selected to illustrate her analysis, as well as in the narrative, Dora V. Smith reflects her awareness of the beauty and power of words to convey feelings and thoughts. In this respect, especially, the study itself is a worthy setting for the contributions of children's authors which have opened new worlds of beauty and imagination to generations of children.

In tracing fifty years of children's literature, the qualities which make a book a genuine "classic" emerge with crystal clarity:

— Characterization true to life, vivid and real
— Plots that are plausible, even when hilarious
— The harmonizing of the world of the imagination and the world of reality into one world
— The happy association of illustration and text so that together they tell a story
— Authorship which depicts genuine knowledge of the subject and personal feelings about it
— Illustrations which alone provide a rich art education for children growing toward maturity
— Language which develops an appreciation of words and appropriateness in their use.

Students of children's literature will find a treasure trove of information in *Fifty Years of Children's Books* related to:

— Changing concepts of books and their role in the development of children
— The development of fascinating publishing trends
— The full flowering of cooperative action by educational organizations, creators of children's books, publishers, and users to assure products of high quality
— The selection of books in order to bring together the right book for the right child at the right moment.

Fifty Years of Children's Books is a distinguished contribution to adults who believe in the power of books to affect the lives of children by one who knows full well how to make words bend to her will.

— Muriel Crosby
Wilmington, Delaware
January, 1963

Fifty Years of Children's Books
1910-1960: Trends, Backgrounds, and Influences

DORA V. SMITH

It is fitting after the fiftieth anniversary of the National Council of Teachers of English that we should pause to consider the course which children's books and reading have followed during the last half century. What the children are reading is intimately associated with the temper of the times, and its influence upon the future may well help to determine the shape of things to come.

Fortunately for the purposes of this study the first *Children's Catalog* appeared in 1909. I found myself asking with lively curiosity what the children were reading in 1910.

The Children's Book World of 1910

MORAL TALES FROM EARLIER GENERATIONS

Boys and girls who have grown up in the last fifty years are more fortunate than they know. They have been spared the "good godly" books of the Puritans. The sin complex was all but gone in 1910—almost, but not quite. *Elsie Dinsmore* (1867) by Martha Finley (pseudonym Martha Farquharson)[1] and *The Wide, Wide World* (1851) by Susan Warner (pseud. Elizabeth Wetherell) were still favorites among the girls. Elsie, you remember, ran through innumerable volumes—childhood, girlhood, wifehood, motherhood, and widowhood, ending with her experiences as a grandmother. In all such books godly children reformed their elders, wept their way through one fit of remorse after another, and came out morally triumphant in the end. One child expressed her supreme joy in reading *Elsie* by announcing, "It was a keen book. I began to cry on the first page."

By 1910 the didactic period in books for children was decidedly on the wane. Jacob Abbott's *Rollo*[2] books in which incident fol-

1

lowed incident for the instruction of the hero in manners, morals, history, and geography were still sufficiently familiar in 1875 to permit Dotty Dimple[3] to observe little blind children in school dramatizing *Rollo on the Atlantic*.[4] Rollo's reaction to what he saw on the other side of the ocean showed that he had learned his lesson well. His youthful exuberance and pride in his own country were reflected in his return "with the satisfied consciousness of hailing from a land superior to those inhabited by foreigners."[5]

Peter Parley records similar sentiments at the close of his *Tales* about Europe, Africa, and Asia:

> We returned satisfied that we are a plain, common-sense people, living on terms of great equality with each other and more distinguished for general intelligence, simple manners, and a good opinion of ourselves.[6]

The end of the characterization was doubtless accurate. Alice M. Jordan, in her delightful commentaries in *From Rollo to Tom Sawyer,* said of the series: "The *Rollo* books had no plot. Incident followed incident, and the story ended when the author was ready to stop."[7]

Clarence Day, reminiscing about his childhood, "when the atmosphere of children's books was thick with nobility," records the influence on an earlier generation of Mrs. Mary Louisa Molesworth's *The Christmas Child* (1880), presented to him on his seventh birthday:

According to Mrs. Molesworth, Ted was always "a boy of nice feelings. Not rough and knock-about in his ways like many schoolboys," she added, in what I felt was a reproving tone, directed at me. He did have a fight with another boy named Rex in one chapter, but he felt it was "so horrid" to hit Rex that he ended by kissing him.

Ted worried about this kissing business afterward and went to his mother. "Was that unmanly, Mother?" he asked.

His mother drew him toward her and looked lovingly into his anxious face. "Unmanly, my boy? No indeed," she said. "Kindness and goodness can never be unmanly." And Ted went off to bed.

I was disturbed by this incident. It made goodness seem more foreign to me than ever. But it deeply moved Mrs. Molesworth. She admired Ted so much that she kept saying so, in little asides to her readers: "I think he had a sweet, brave spirit, don't you, children?" she said in this chapter; and she went on to describe how considerate and patient he was, and how "he was never guilty of any rudeness." It was plain that Ted had all the virtues.

Ted died at the end of the book, just before his twelfth birthday. Very good children often did die on the last page, I had noticed. They never had anything very violent or awful the matter with them, they just took sick and expired very gently of some vague and unnamed disease.[8]

Echoes of the same point of view in books for girls could be found in Maria Edgeworth's *Moral Tales* (1801) and in her earlier *The Parent's Assistant* (1796). In "The Purple Jar," for instance, which first appeared in the latter, Little Rosamond was left to exercise her own moral judgment as to whether she should buy a beautiful purple glass jar or a much needed pair of shoes. She chose the purple jar, only to find that its gorgeous color came from purple water shining through the glass. In the end, she paid for her impracticality by staying home from the Crystal Palace exhibition because there were too many holes in her shoes.

GIRLS—IN SERIES AND OUT

It wasn't long, however, before lively, entertaining girls were substituted for Rosamond and Elsie in the interminable series, a rash of which broke out at the turn of the century. What girl of that period does not have nostalgic recollections of *Dotty Dimple,*[9] *What Katy Did at Home, What Katy Did at School,* and for want of a more specific title, *What Katy Did Next?*[10]

Five Little Peppers and How They Grew presented idyllic family life.[11] Then there were the Little Colonel and her friends—and also her yardstick, which she carried through life in search of the boy who could measure up and become her husband. Finally, he appeared in the romantic volume entitled *Little Colonel's Knight Comes Riding.*[12] I have a friend who insists that the reason she is not married is that she carried the Little Colonel's yardstick too long and never found the man who could qualify.

Then there were the *Hildegarde* books[13] and *The Three Margarets*[14] and a host of other stories of girls who exemplified the qualities of a perfect lady although the author did not specifically enumerate them. Comparison of these growing girls with Carol Brink's Caddie Woodlawn or with Elizabeth Speare's heroine in *The Witch of Blackbird Pond* (1958) reveals clearly how reality has crept into the better books of our day.

As forerunners of the latter, however, the girls had Louisa May Alcott's *Little Women* (1868); Edith Nesbit's Bastable children in *The Story of the Treasure Seekers* (1899), *The Would-Be-Goods* (1901), and *The New Treasure Seekers* (1904); and Kate Douglas Wiggin's *Rebecca of Sunnybrook Farm* (1903). Equally popular for their Pollyanna attitudes and homespun virtues were Lucy M. Montgomery's *Anne of Green Gables* (1908) and Alice Hegan Rice's *Mrs. Wiggs of the Cabbage Patch* (1901). Akin to Mrs. Wiggs's homely virtues were those of the Ruggles family in the tearful story of *The Birds' Christmas Carol* (1887) by Kate Douglas Wiggin.

THE SWASHBUCKLING HEROES

The "noble" boys represented by Rollo, by *The Christmas Child* (1880), and by *Little Lord Fauntleroy* (1886) were followed by a crowd of swashbuckling fellows whose loyalty was to flag and to country. The *Children's Catalog* in 1909 was filled with stories of vigorous battles on land and sea, in which American boys took on Indians, foreign invaders, phantom vessels, grizzlies, or their brothers on one side or other of the Mason-Dixon line. George Grinnell's *Jack among the Indians* (1900) was a great favorite along with Henry H. Clark's *Joe Bentley,*

Naval Cadet (1889) and Everett T. Tomlinson's *Boy Soldiers of 1812* (1895).[15] If the hero was the age of the reader, so much the better.

But the prime favorites were the Henty books, for George Henty had been a war correspondent in the British army and his heroes roamed the world—*Under Drake's Flag* (1883), for example, or *With Kitchener in the Soudan* (1903). You remember the preparations of Little Miss Muffet and Spider for entertaining the storybook characters in Samuel McChord Crothers's *Miss Muffet's Christmas Party* (1902)? As the invitation list grew longer and longer, Spider said in consternation, "But what about Mr. Henty's boys? There are so many of them."

"There *seem* to be a great many of them," said Miss Muffet, "but I've sometimes thought that there may be only two, only they live in different centuries and go to different wars."

Spider thought they could easily change their names without changing their characters. "So an invitation was sent to Ronald Leslie, alias Wulf, Roger, Lionel, Stanley, etc., On the Firing Line, Near Carthage, Quebec, Crécy, Waterloo, Khartoum, or wherever the Enemy may be found in Force."[16]

SCHOOL STORIES, ADVENTURE, AND ROBINSONADES

But there were more normal boys, also, like those in Thomas Hughes's *Tom Brown's*

School Days (1857), in Thomas Bailey Aldrich's *The Story of a Bad Boy* (1870), in James O. Kaler's *Toby Tyler or Ten Weeks with a Circus* (1881), and in Edward Eggleston's *The Hoosier School-Boy* (1883). Then came Samuel L. Clemens's *The Adventures of Tom Sawyer* (1876), joined some years later by *The Adventures of Huckleberry Finn* (1885). "These two," said an English critic, "are attached to the Mississippi, but they are a part of the world."[17] Kipling's *Captains Courageous* (1897) added a new setting to stories of boy life, and Arthur S. Pier produced his boarding school story, *The Boys of St. Timothy's* (1904).

So was there also exciting fiction, some of it Robinsonades in the wake of Robinson Crusoe in *The Life and Strange Surprizing Adventures of the Renowned Hero, Robinson Crusoe, of York, Mariner* (1719). Among these were Johann Wyss's *The Swiss Family Robinson*, first translated into English in 1814; Frederick Marryat's *Masterman Ready* (1841-42); and Robert Louis Stevenson's *Treasure Island* (1883). In very different tone was Richard Henry Dana's *Two Years before the Mast* (1840), a realistic account of the boredom, cruelty, and daily experiences of men in the merchant marine. *Gulliver's Travels* by Jonathan Swift (then called *Travels into Several Remote Nations of the World. In Four Parts. By Lemuel Gulliver*). was available in 1726 and in a children's edition in the United States by James Baldwin as early as 1908.

THE "IMMORTAL FOUR"

The last quarter of the nineteenth century saw the tremendous spread of cheap, tawdry fiction, akin to the dime novel, one hundred or more books written according to an established pattern by a single author. Caroline Hewins, from her vantage point as librarian of the Young Men's Institute in Hartford, Connecticut, struck out against "the immortal four."[18] They were Martha Finley (pseud. Martha Farquharson), author of the *Elsie* books; Horatio Alger, Jr.; William Taylor Adams, popularly known as Oliver Optic; and Charles Austin Fosdick, who wrote under the name of Harry Castlemon. Horatio Alger's errand boys who carved new roads to fortune were bombastic heroes setting forth false values.[19] Oliver Optic, a school principal, had written one hundred and sixteen books in cloth bindings exclusive of those he had produced in paper, among them his *Young America Abroad* series, filled with drunken youths at sea, gambling, pillaging, and stealing.[20] Harry Castlemon's *Frank on a Gunboat* (1865), *Frank on the Lower Mississippi* (1867), and the like harked back to the days when the author had run away from home to join the navy during the Civil War.[21] Miss Hewins worked through letters to the press, talks to parents, and, above all, through vigorous promotion of better books to offset the influence of the series.

"MILE-A-MINUTE" FICTION FOR BOYS AND THE FIRST NATIONAL BOOK WEEK

Then came the syndicate for mass produc-tion of cheap juveniles. Tom Swift celebrated his fiftieth anniversary in 1960, having apparently thrown down the glove to English teachers and librarians as early as 1910. His first inventions were a motorcycle, an electric runabout, an airship, and a submarine (1910). Today, Tom Swift Junior is busy in the caves of nuclear fire (1956) and with his ultrasonic cycloplane (1957), with the cosmic astronauts (1960) and with a visitor from Mars (1961). In 1908 Edward Stratemeyer had formed his syndicate to turn out boys' books on a mass production basis.[22] He used at least thirteen different names. Among others, he was Arthur Winfield, author of the *Rover Boys*,[23] Clarence Young, writer of the *Motor Boys* series,[24] Victor Appleton, inventor of *Tom Swift*;[25] and Laura Lee Hope, creator of *The Bobbsey Twins*.[26] "He wrote some one hundred and sixty books under syndicate pseudonyms, fifty or so under his own name, and devised plots for about eight hundred others which were farmed out to hired hacks."[27]

Franklin K. Mathiews, librarian of the Boy Scouts of America, toured the country just before the opening of World War I and came back exceedingly conscious of the need of better books for boys: "In almost all of this 'mile-a-minute' fiction," he said, "some inflammable tale of improbable adventure is told. Boys rise on aeroplanes [1916] as easily as though on bicycles; criminals are captured by them with a facility that matches the ability of Sherlock Holmes; and when it comes to getting on in the world, the cleverness of these hustling boys is comparable only to those captains of industry and Napoleons of finance, who have made millions in a minute."[28] He believed in the exercise of the imagination as an aid to wholesome development, but he wanted it to "stimulate initiative and awaken such resourcefulness as will aid the boy to change capacity into capability."[29]

On behalf of this kind of reading guidance, he persuaded Frederic G. Melcher and the American Association of Book Publishers to establish the first National Children's Book Week in 1919 in order "to bring together in common cause the many groups which had a deep interest in the reading of children—librarians, teachers, publishers, artists, authors, scout leaders, and the like."[30]

NEIGHBORS AROUND THE WORLD

Stories of other lands came largely in series. It was Horace Scudder (unless one considers Rollo a forerunner of the Bodleys) who first introduced the new travel books for children with his Bodley family who "Afoot," "On Wheels," and "Abroad" (1875-1880) combined learning with entertainment in their family ventures into New England, Holland, and the Scandinavian countries.[31] As in our own day, the search for ancestors in Europe added a personal motive to their travels.

Hezekiah Butterworth's *Zigzag Journeys* (1880-1895) had opened up the field in the eighties and nineties,[32] followed by the *Little Journeys* series (1900-1911) which persisted in new editions until 1931.[33] The first decade of the new century saw the flowering of *The Boy Travellers* (1880-1928),[34] the *Little People Everywhere* series (1909-1916),[35] *Peeps at Many Lands* (1907-1933),[36] and, most popular of all, the *Our Little Cousins* series (1901-1930) by Mary Wade and others.[37] In general, the *Our Little Cousins* books gave "fairly accurate information in a style without distinction, accompanied by illustrations of little merit."[38] However, they apparently had real interest for children and gave them information which they could read for themselves.

Books such as these, which followed the rush of immigration of the 1890's, stemmed from a recognition of the varied backgrounds of the American people and a desire to give children an appreciation of them. Certain of the *Our Little Cousins* series centered in somewhat lifelike characters which paved the way in the decades to come for stories of children of real personality. Mrs. Johanna Spyri's *Heidi* (1884) and Mary Mapes Dodge's *Hans Brinker* (1866) had already shown what could be done to make children of other lands human and individual. However, comparison of *Hans Brinker* with Meindert De Jong's recent *The Wheel on the School* (1954) will perhaps reveal why the Dutch prefer to be represented by De Jong's book rather than by *Hans Brinker*, by William Griffis's *Brave Little Holland and What She Taught Us* (1894), or even by the small boy who held back the North Atlantic by thrusting his tiny finger into the leak in the dike.[39] Stories with specific geographical backgrounds and individual characters were beginning to appear, however, in Mrs. Josephine Peary's *Snow Baby* (1901) and in Hans Aanrud's *Lisbeth Longfrock* (1907).

With little children, a prime favorite at the turn of the century was *The Seven Little Sisters Who Live on the Round Ball That Floats in the Air*, written forty years earlier by Jane Andrews. To them the "little brown baby" whose mother "tossed her up into her little swinging bed in the tree" and sang her a "mild sweet song," until she fell asleep was as real as the children next door.[40] So also was Agoonack, the Esquimau sister whose round, fat, greasy little face looked out from a white shaggy bearskin hood and whose great brick oven of a house opened the reader's eyes to the fact that life is different for children in various parts of the world. But the American child was always outside looking in at modes of living and children that were curiously different. How changed the point of view was to become in the better children's books of the 1930's!

A GLORIFIED AMERICA AND THE WESTWARD TREK

By the last quarter of the nineteenth century, the United States had become exceedingly conscious of its vast resources and of its possibilities as an independent nation. Writers for children had transmitted with adolescent assurance their optimism and pride in their country. History had become largely the boisterous story of triumphant battles on land and sea, of the unmatched prowess and selfless devotion of our national heroes. More than one hundred tales of naval exploits alone appeared in the first *Children's Catalog* (1909). A similar array of stories of battles on land had presented dramatically to American youth the ideal of the heroic sacrifice of life in devotion to duty. Charles C. Coffin's *The Boys of '76* (1877) was among the most popular of these stories. Its dedication is significant: "To my nephews, whose ancestors took part in the battles of the Revolution." The same spirit had been fostered in popular books of ballads and poems like Brander Matthews's *Poems of American Patriotism* (1882) and David Montgomery's *Heroic Ballads* (1890).

The westward trek had afforded another area of romance and heroism. Children had been fortunate at the midcentury to have Francis Parkman's *The California and Oregon Trail* (1849) with its graphic account of the young Bostonian's adventures with four companions on the road west, encountering Indians, buffalo, and many hardships along the way—a vivid personalized introduction to the westward movement, told with a distinctly literary flavor. By the last decade of the nineteenth century, such writers as Everett T. Tomlinson, Elbridge S. Brooks, William O. Stoddard, and Wilbur Fisk Gordy had joined the promoters of America's glory. Even John Fiske, the noted historian, had added to the collection histories which aimed to show that "a guiding Providence had from the very start directed America on her successful course."[41] At the same time, Thomas Janvier, in another area of history, had written his *The Aztec Treasure House* (1890) recounting the search for the lost city of the ancient Aztecs, which, in the form of an exciting adventure story, had introduced children to the place of the archeologist in historical research.

By 1907 Joseph Altsheler was writing for boys and girls tales of the Civil War and of Indian fighters of Kentucky and the way west. His stories, though slight, were full of vigor and a certain truth to historical backgrounds, which made *The Young Trailers* (1907) and *The Horsemen of the Plains* (1910) prime favorites among average readers for years to come.[42] James Fenimore Cooper had earlier presented a romanticized picture of the Indian in *The Last of the Mohicans* (1826) although, as Irvin Cobb later pointed out, from the boys' point of view, "his Indians were everlastingly slow about getting under way with their scalping operations."[43]

THE ROMANCE OF HISTORY ABROAD

At the same time, England was being featured in historical fiction of a similar kind. The popularity of George A. Henty's dramatic adventure stories of the farflung battles for the Empire has already been mentioned. A romantic touch had been given to history for girls in the sentimental stories of Charlotte M. Yonge—*Richard the Fearless, or The Little Duke* (1856), for example, which revealed the childhood of the youthful Duke of Normandy, and *The Dove in the Eagle's Nest* (1866), which presented the life of a little girl growing up in the castle of a robber baron.

From *The Merry Adventures of Robin Hood of Great Renown in Nottinghamshire* by Howard Pyle. Il. by author. Scribner, 1946.

Sidney Lanier's edition of *The Boy's Froissart*, which had appeared in 1879, and his similar volume of Sir Thomas Malory's

8

The Boy's King Arthur (1880) had served to whet the appetite of young readers for stories of knightly adventure. Howard Pyle had brought to life the lusty outlaws of Sherwood Forest in his superbly detailed pictures and robust narrative of *The Merry Adventures of Robin Hood of Great Renown in Nottinghamshire* (1883, revised 1946). His less romantic *Men of Iron* (1891) had added something of the grimness which life held for the knightly followers of King Richard during the reign of Henry the Fourth. Sir Arthur Conan Doyle's *The White Company* (1891) had revealed the prowess of the English bowmen in fourteenth century France and Castile.

TRENDS IN THE WRITING OF HISTORY

Gradually careful research began to play a part in historical writing for children. In 1906, for example, Helen Nicolay's *The Boy's Life of Abraham Lincoln* had appeared. The author, a recognized scholar, had participated in the research for her father's ten-volume work on Lincoln. She wrote clear, straightforward prose and respected the intelligence of youthful readers. Historians like Eva March Tappan had begun to present history as more than a series of battles or even of historical events and to center attention on the manner of living and thinking of a people, on their social and economic development, and on the many contributions of art, literature, and invention to the advance of civilization. Her *The Story of the Greek People* (1908) is an early example of a movement in the writing of history which developed in the decades to follow.

In 1907 there came from France Boutet de Monvel's *Joan of Arc,* a story for children which, years before its time, revealed the perfect harmony of illustration and text which was to characterize the Golden Age of picture books from 1925 on. Full-page illustrations and sometimes double-page spreads told the story with a broad sweep of action. Though the details never interfered with the total impact of the scene, they presented a minute picture of chivalry in fifteenth century France—its ceremonials, its castles, its heraldic trappings, and its methods of warfare, which children pored over by the hour.

NATURE STORIES—A PERSONIFIED WORLD

Nature books in 1910 ranged from the ultrasentimental, which commonly gave to plants, trees, and animals both the intelligence and the speech of human beings, to the strictly informative. Library shelves were filled with *The Stories Mother Nature Told Her Children* (1889) and tales of the protecting care of *Old Mother West Wind* (1910) for her little ones, as told by Thornton W. Burgess fifty years ago. Even Samuel Scudder gave to his serious though chatty book about butterflies the popular title of *Frail Children of the Air* (1895).

Miss Andrews's introduction to her *The Stories Mother Nature Told Her Children* revealed the point of view of many science books in 1889:

Do you know Mother Nature? She it is to whom God has given the care of the earth, and all that grows upon it, just as He has given to your mother the care of her family of boys and girls.

You may think that Mother Nature, like the famous "old woman who lived in the shoe," has so many children that she doesn't know what to do. But you will know better when you become acquainted with her, and learn how strong she is and how active; how she can really be in fifty places at once taking care of a sick tree, or a baby flower just born; and at the same time, building underground palaces, guiding the steps of little travellers setting out on long journeys, and sweeping, dusting, and arranging her great house—the earth.[44]

As late as 1910, Thornton Burgess's *Old Mother West Wind* continued to personify the elements of nature:

Old Mother West Wind came down from the Purple Hills in the golden light of the early morning. Over her shoulders was slung a bag—a great big bag—and in the bag were all of Old Mother West Wind's children, the Merry Little Breezes. When she reached the green meadows, Old Mother West Wind opened her bag, turned it upside down and shook it. Out tumbled all the Merry Little Breezes and began to spin round and round for very joy, for you see they were to play in the Green Meadows all day long until Old Mother West Wind should come back at night and take them all to their home behind the Purple Hills. . . .

The Merry Little Breezes raced across the Green Meadows to the Smiling Pool to say good morning to Grandfather Frog, who sat on a big lily pad watching for green flies for breakfast. . . .

"What's the news, Grandfather Frog?" they cried.

"Mrs. Redwing has a new speckled egg in her nest in the bulrushes," said Grandfather Frog.

"We must see it," cried the Merry Little Breezes, and away they all ran to the swamp where the bulrushes grow.

Now someone else had heard of Mrs. Redwing's little nest in the bulrushes, and he had started out bright and early that morning to try to find it, for he wanted to steal the little speckled eggs just because they were pretty. It was Tommy Brown, the farmer's boy.

When the Merry Little Breezes reached the swamp where the bulrushes grow they found poor Mrs. Redwing in great distress. She was afraid that Tommy Brown would find her little nest, for he was very, very near it, and his eyes were very, very sharp.

"Oh," cried the Merry Little Breezes, "we must help Mrs. Redwing save her pretty speckled eggs from bad Tommy Brown!"

So one of the Merry Little Breezes whisked Tommy Brown's old straw hat off his head over into the Green Meadows. Of course Tommy ran after it. Just as he stooped to pick it up another little Breeze ran away with it. Then they took turns, first one little Breeze, then another little Breeze, then another little Breeze running away with the old straw hat just as Tommy Brown would almost get his hands on it. Down past the Smiling Pool and across the Laughing Brook they raced and chased the old straw hat, Tommy Brown running after it, very cross, very red in the face, and breathing very hard. Way across the Green Meadows they ran to the edge of the wood, where they hung the old straw hat in the middle of a thorn tree. By the time Tommy Brown had it once more on his head he had forgotten all about Mrs. Redwing and her little nest. . . .

And all the Merry Breezes danced away across the Green Meadows to the swamp where the bulrushes grow to see the new speckled egg in the little nest where Mrs. Redwing was singing for joy. And while she sang, the Merry Little Breezes danced among the bulrushes, for they knew, and Mrs. Redwing knew, that someday out of that pretty speckled egg would come a wee baby Redwing." [45]

ANIMALS IN FACT AND FICTION

However, between 1898 and 1904 authentic and realistic treatments of nature and animals had appeared in school editions of the works of notable writers in the field of science; for example, Frank Chapman's *Bird-Life* (1897), Harriet Miller's (pseud. Olive T. Miller) *First Book of Birds* (1899), John Burroughs's *Squirrels and Other Fur-Bearers* (1900), Albert Bigelow Paine's *Hollow Tree and Deep Woods Book* (1901), Charles C. G. D. Roberts's *Kindred of the Wild* (1902), David Starr Jordan's *True Tales of Birds and Beasts* (1902), and Anna B. Comstock's *Ways of the Six-Footed* (1903). Popular fiction accompanying this upsurge of interest in wild life was adopted by the boys as their own: Ernest Thompson Seton's *Wild Animals I Have Known* (1898) and *Monarch, the Big Bear of Tallac* (1904) and Jack London's *Call of the Wild* (1903). Their sentimental counterparts in Anna Sewell's *Black Beauty* (subtitled "The Uncle Tom's Cabin of the Horse") (1891) and Marshall Saunders's *Beautiful Joe* (1894) were popular with both boys and girls.

Themes related to science were the subject of several famous books of fiction of the same period. Jules Verne's *Twenty Thousand Leagues under the Sea* (1873), a fantasy of amazing scientific and technical achievements, has proved strangely prophetic of later inventions. Verne has been called the father of science fiction. Perhaps more farfetched as an aspect of science is Sir Arthur Conan Doyle's *Adventures of Sherlock Holmes* (1892), but it was clever storytelling and was equally popular with boys and men.

IMAGINATIVE LITERATURE FOR CHILDREN

The heritage of the classics. At the turn of the century children were rich in imaginative literature. They had Charles Lamb's *Tales from Shakespear* designed for the Use of Young Persons (1807) and "Rip Van Winkle" and "The Legend of Sleepy Hollow" from Washington Irving's *The Sketch Book* (1819-20). In 1865 *Alice's Adventures in Wonderland* by Charles Dodgson (pseud. Lewis Carroll) had arrived to take top place in the literature of fantasy. Three years later George Macdonald had produced his moving story of the little boy, Diamond, *At the Back of the North Wind* (1871). Joel Chandler Harris, in 1880, had recorded for American children the folklore of the Negro in *Uncle Remus: His Songs and Sayings.* More humor had followed in *The Adventures of Pinocchio* (1892) by Carlo Lorenzini (pseud. C. Collodi), Italy's gift to English-speaking children.[46] *Pinocchio* had been followed two years later by Kipling's inimitable *Jungle Books* (1894-95) and in 1902 by *The Just So Stories*. Meanwhile, Joseph Jacobs had given English-speaking children *The Fables of Aesop* (1889), and Andrew Lang had collected and edited for them *Arabian Nights Entertainments* (1898).[47]

Among the most popular collections of literature for children in the early years of the twentieth century had been Kate Douglas Wiggin and Nora Archibald Smith's *The Fairy Ring* (1906) and *Tales of Laughter* (1908). By 1907 Selma Lagerlöf's *The Wonderful Adventures of Nils* had proved that folklore, the natural beauties, and the geography of a land like Sweden could be woven into a fantasy of great charm. Kenneth Grahame's *The Wind in the Willows* had

From *The Wind in the Willows* by Kenneth Grahame. Il. by Ernest H. Shepard. Scribner, 1960. ©1933, 1961 Ernest H. Shepard.

appeared in 1908. Like the National Council of Teachers of English, it recently celebrated

its first half century, in this case with a beautiful new edition containing several additional pictures in color by its famous illustrator, Ernest H. Shepard. "What gives this tale its enduring quality," says Frances Clark Sayers in her introduction to the new edition, "is the depth of feeling which the author brings to it; the extent of his own commitment to the world he here creates. For this is a world complete in itself, with a distinctive aura, its characters creatures of immense individuality."[48] As the reader follows Toad and Rat through the six new full-page illustrations in color, he remembers the last injunction of Kenneth Grahame, when, too old to accompany Mr. Shepard to the meadow and the stream, he pointed in the direction of the little creatures and said, "Be kind to them."[49] Children should not fail to hear the rhythmic and poetic prose of *The Wind in the Willows* read aloud by their teachers.

Myths and hero stories. Hero stories, myths, and legends of Greece and Rome were available in excellent editions for the children of 1910. Nathaniel Hawthorne's *A Wonder-Book for Girls and Boys* (1852) had presented the fabulous stories of "The Golden Touch," "The Gorgon's Head," and "The Chimera"; whereas *Tanglewood Tales* (1853) had offered the exploits of Theseus and the minotaur, Cadmus and the dragon's teeth, and Jason and the golden fleece. Kingsley's *The Heroes* (1855) had dealt with many of the same heroes, to whom Josephine Peabody had added additional gods and heroes in *Old Greek Folk-Stories Told Anew* (1897). By the first decade of the twentieth century Alfred J. Church, a classical scholar of the day, had rewritten for children the stories of Homer in *The Odyssey for Boys and Girls* (1906) and *The Iliad for Boys and Girls* (1907). *The Aeneid* of Virgil was retold in the same series (1908).

Fairy tales. The fairy tales had been available in English for half a century or more. Charles Perrault's *Tales of Mother Goose* was introduced into England from France, probably in 1729, "with some high support of fashion."[50] Wilhelm and Jacob Grimm's *German Popular Stories* had appeared in 1823, and Hans Christian Andersen's *Wonderful Stories for Children* was translated in 1846 by Mrs. Mary Howitt and published by Chapman and Hall.[51] Peter C. Asbjörnsen and Jörgen E. Moe's *Popular Tales from the Norse* had reached England in 1859, and Joseph Jacobs's *English Fairy Tales* had been published in London in 1890. Seumas McManus's *Donegal Fairy Stories* had completed the list in 1901. "We had most of the tongues of Europe speaking to our children," wrote an English critic, recording the triumph of fairy lore over morals and instruction.[52] And what girl has ever forgotten her prolonged trek through the "color" books of Andrew Lang (1889-1910),[53] recently clad in fresh color by their publisher (Longmans, 1947-1949)?

The Peterkins. In a class all by themselves were the Peterkins, who had come out of New England in 1880. Such was their spirit of "togetherness" that they listened to each other ad infinitum until they were unable to decide on a solution to any problem until the practical Lady from Philadelphia saw the obvious and set them right. Both humor and characterization had taken a new and delightful turn in children's books with the arrival on the scene of Lucretia Hale's book.

Mother Goose and the nursery tales. Prior to 1910 there had been little in books for young children, but that little had been very important. Mother Goose and the nursery rhymes had given British and American children a treasure unsurpassed in any country in the world.[54] Illustrations of nursery tales and rhymes by Walter Crane, by Randolph Caldecott, by Kate Greenaway, by L. Leslie Brooke, and by Howard Pyle, most of which had come out between the years 1876 and 1910, are not to be matched anywhere. "With them," write the authors of *A Critical History of Children's Literature,* "we find for the first time, color used with skill and imagination to make children's books truly a thing of beauty."[55] The bold outlines and clear primitive colors of Walter Crane's picture books—such as *The Baby's Opera, The Baby's Bouquet,* and *Goody Two Shoes Picture Book*—with their decorative borders, harmoniously designed, had opened up a whole new world of illustration.[56] Randolph Caldecott had run the full gamut from his "headlong, horn-blowing, cheek-bursting huntsmen" (to borrow a phrase from L. Leslie Brooke) to the delicate grace and ridiculous gentlemanliness of *A Frog He*

Would A-Wooing Go (Caldecott Picture Books, 1878-84).[57]

These two had soon been joined by Howard Pyle with his gay verses and spirited tales in *Pepper and Salt* (1885), its chief purpose being to give children a chance to "laugh and be merry."[58] Three years later had come *The Wonder Clock* (1888). In both, the author had demonstrated his dual power as storyteller and artist. At this time, too, Kate Greenaway had appeared with her quaint, mob-capped little girls and her dainty Eton-jacketed boys at play in pleasant English gardens (*A Apple Pie,* 1886).[59]

Peter Rabbit. Then, to make the children's joy complete, Beatrix Potter had produced Peter Rabbit (1903) and the other lovable little creatures of the English Lake Country, whose gently human qualities reflected the child's own experiences and attitudes. The children immediately took them to their hearts, and they have been there ever since. Next had come L. Leslie Brooke and his quietly irresistible chuckle. His three luscious pigs (contrast them with Walt Disney's if you want to see how delightful they really are), each with a personality of his own, and the inimitable family of the three bears make *The Golden Goose Book* (1905) a must for every child's library. The bears have since been an answer to at least one boy's remonstrance against another illustrator's pictures for the same story: "These bears are not a family; they are just colored to match the rest of the picture."[60] Leslie Brooke's bubbling humor came often from little unexpected details and slight incidents improvised to interpret character or scene; for example, the chairs embroidered with bees in the home of the bears and with acorns in the home of the pigs, or the irrepressible baby bear on the last page of the story, out for a walk and proudly wearing Goldilocks' lost hat—backwards!

Poetry—solemn and not so solemn. In poetry, the children of 1910 had, besides five centuries of English verse and the standard poets of New England's flowering, certain books of their very own: William Blake's *Songs of Innocence* (1789), Clement Moore's *A Visit from St. Nicholas* (1823),[61] Christina Rossetti's *Sing-Song* (1872), Jane and Ann Taylor's *Little Ann and Other Poems* (1883), Edward Lear's *Nonsense Books* (1888), Eugene Field's *Songs of Childhood* (1897), James Whitcomb Riley's *Rhymes of Childhood* (1891), and Frank D. Sherman's *Little-Folk Lyrics* (1897). Kate Greenaway had also illustrated for them Browning's *The Pied Piper of Hamelin* (1888).

It is interesting to note that not a single anthology available in 1909 remains in the *Children's Catalog* of 1961.[62] Several English writers had brought out collections of verse for children. William E. Henley's *Lyra Heroica; A Book of Verse for Boys* (1891) had been highly recommended as "a book of 'Noble Numbers' chosen to set forth the beauty and joy of living, the beauty and blessedness of death, the glory of battle and adventure, the nobility of devotion—to a cause, an ideal, a passion, even—the dignity of resistance, the sacred quality of patriotism."[63] It contained, together with a scattering of older ballads, standard English verse from Michael Drayton's "Agincourt" through George Herbert's "Memento Mori" to poems by Wordsworth, Browning, and Kipling.

E. V. Lucas had called his collection of poems *A Book of Verses for Children* (1897). The selections were to be "a 'stepping-stone' to the better thing."[64] In spite of a preponderance of moralistic verse, the volume had the merit of topical arrangement rather than chronological order by authors, so that poems could be related to the interests of children—"Dogs," "Horses," "Open Air," and the like. "Poets at Play" was the unique title of the section of humorous verse. A generous sprinkling of "story" poems must have pleased the young readers.

With some truth, Louey Chisholm had remarked in the introduction to her popular collection called *The Golden Staircase* that previous compilers had "a more intimate acquaintance with poetry than with boys and girls. . . . The first qualification for the task," she believed, "is love and knowledge of the little readers."[65] Her aim had been to give children enjoyment of "merriment, beauty, and heroism." The two hundred poems were arranged in order of difficulty, maturity of interest, and appeal to children of increasing ages from four to fourteen. Moralistic poems like "Who Stole the Birds' Nest" and "The Story of Augustus Who Would Not Have Any Soup" (he died as a result) along with "How Doth the Little Busy Bee" and "Great, Wide, Beautiful, Wonderful World" mingled with the poetry of Scott, Shakespeare, Tennyson, Jane and Ann Taylor, Stevenson, and Allingham.

Meanwhile, Kate Douglas Wiggin and her sister, Nora Archibald Smith, had brought out two of the most popular collections of the first decade of the twentieth century: *Golden Numbers* (1903) for the upper grades and *The Posy Ring* (1903) for little children. Both had been carefully selected with a good balance between mature quality and less well known poems suitable for children. Both were grouped under topics attractive to young readers—in *Golden Numbers* such headings as "On the Wing," "The New World and Old Glory," or "In Merry Mood," and in *The Posy Ring*, "Hiawatha's Chickens," "Play-Time," "Story-Time," and "Bed-Time." Both contained a goodly number of narrative poems.

High standards of selection from traditional verse make *Golden Numbers* very challenging reading for older pupils. The editors' plea to their youthful readers was that they begin with the poems which would give them immediate pleasure and then go on to those which challenged their highest powers. In the edition which followed twenty-six years later, they reemphasized this point with the story of the scholarly minister who was forced to preach to an uneducated congregation. When asked how he met the challenge, he replied: "I try to be very simple a part of the time, but not always; about once a month I fling the fodder so high in the rack that no man can catch a single straw without stretching his neck!"[66] Apparently the problems of teaching poetry have not changed much since the century opened.

There were no pictures in any of the volumes discussed in the preceding paragraphs. Lucas's later collection, *Another Book of Verses,* which came out in 1907, contained charming drawings by Francis Bedford, introducing each section of the book. All of these anthologies were in actuality reference sources or "mothers' helpers" rather than books which children themselves could handle with ease.

The classics in sets. Certain sets of children's classics had also appeared in forms which younger readers could more readily handle by themselves—*The Heart of Oak Books* (1903), for example, a literary series by Charles Eliot Norton, which appeared in seven volumes, graded for use in home and school, and Hamilton Wright Mabie's *Every Child Should Know* series (1905-13), followed in 1912 by the *Junior Classics.* Horace E. Scudder's *The Children's Book* (1881) had served as a guide to parents of an earlier generation. It was revised in 1903 and again in 1910.

The Period of Transition—1910-1925

MORE LITERATURE FOR CHILDREN

The years from 1910 to 1925 were in many ways a transition period, paving the way for the flowering of children's books after World War I.

Fairy, folk, and hero stories. In the realm of fairy, folk, and hero stories, more "tongues" were speaking to our children. Judge Parry's retelling of Miguel de Cervantes's *Don Quixote of the Mancha* (1909, new 1911) with illustrations by Walter Crane made its irresistible humor accessible to children as it had never been before. Eleanor Hull gave *The Boys' Cuchulain* (1910) to British and American children. Gudrun Thorne-Thomsen retold the Norwegian stories in *East o' the Sun and West o' the Moon with Other Norwegian Folk Tales* (1912). Ellen C. Babbitt brought the *Jataka Tales* (1912) from India, and Valery Carrick, the *Picture Tales from the Russian* (1913). The latter were especially popular with young children because of their humor and simplicity of plot and illustration. In 1918 Arthur Rackham illustrated Flora A. Steel's *English Fairy Tales.* The trend seemed to be away from Greece and Rome except for Padraic Colum's *The Adventures of Odysseus and the Tale of*

Troy (1918) and *The Golden Fleece and the Heroes Who Lived before Achilles* (1921). Both were beautifully illustrated with sketches by the Hungarian artist, Willy Pogany.

The imaginative story. The second decade of the twentieth century opened propitiously with the arrival of Peter Pan, the boy who never grew up (J. M. Barrie, *Peter and Wendy*, 1911). Children still follow breathlessly his adventures in Never-Never Land as he guides his friends through many whimsical and not-so-whimsical experiences. Ten years after *The Wind in the Willows* came another prose-poem, dealing with the highly emotional and imaginative experiences of a real child in pursuit of a mirage in the untamed lands of South America— *A Little Boy Lost* by W. H. Hudson (1918). This time it was not a mathematician but a poet-naturalist who shared with humor and impressionistic insight his early, almost mystical delight in the wild reaches of the pampas. In the realm of the imaginative story, moreover, the early twenties saw the appearance of Hugh Lofting's *The Voyages of Dr. Dolittle* (1922) and Carl Sandburg's *Rootabaga Stories* (1922). L. Leslie Brooke's *Ring o' Roses* (1923) with its jolly rhythmic pictures to accompany the nursery rhymes brought joy to little children. Meanwhile, Charles J. Finger returned from South America with *Tales from Silver Lands* (1924), and tall tales followed in Esther Shephard's *Paul Bunyan* (1924).

As an earnest of what was soon to hap-pen in the realm of illustration, William Nicholson brought a toy rabbit to life in a series of imaginative lithographs for Margery Bianco's *The Velveteen Rabbit* (1922). C. B. Falls's *A B C Book* came from the press

From *A B C Book* by C. B. Falls. Il. by author. Doubleday, 1923.

in 1923. With its colorful woodcuts of superbly drawn animals and its beautifully shaded alphabet, it remains one of the distinguished books for children produced in this country. It was followed the next year by Margery Clark's *The Poppy Seed Cakes* (1924), the joyous and appealing story of Andrewshek, whose Auntie Katuska came from the Old World to make poppy seed cakes. The gay, colorful illustrations by Maud and Miska Petersham gave promise of things to come.

Mother Goose came to children during this period in simple and attractive format in Blanche Fisher Wright's *The Real Mother Goose* (1916). The clarity and simplicity of the pictures and the combination of bright and soft colors make the edition particularly suitable for little children.

Walter de la Mare and others. Perhaps the greatest gift of these years to poetry for children was Walter de la Mare's *Peacock Pie* (1913) and *A Child's Day* (1915). Up to this time poems about the daily happenings of a child's life had been largely pedestrian in meter and concept, many of them pointing an accusing finger at the untoward behavior of youth. Walter de la Mare delighted in children as he found them, chuckling with them at their whims and foibles. "Poor Tired Tim" is a favorite everywhere. Only a poet who understood the feelings of little girls could possibly have written the introductory lines of *A Child's Day:*

  I sang a song to Rosamond Rose
  Only the wind in the twilight knows:
  I sang a song to Jeanetta Jennie,
  She flung from her window a silver penny:
  I sang a song to Matilda May,
  She took to her heels and ran away:
  I sang a song to Susannah Sue,

She giggled the whole of the verses through:
But nevertheless, as sweet as I can,
I'll sing a song to Elizabeth Ann.[67]

From *Peacock Pie* by Walter de la Mare. Il. by W. Heath Robinson. Constable, n. d.

His confession of what the poem was to be about expresses the credo of much poetry later to be written for children—not to inform or to instruct, but to entertain—while it deepened their insight into human personality and lent a new interest to the things of everyday:

  And all my song is meant to say
  Is just what she did one long, long day
  With her own little self to play with only
  Yet never once felt the least bit lonely.[68]

But Walter de la Mare was equally at home in the natural and the supernatural world. In imagination he led children into the land of "faerie" and opened their eyes and ears to the mystic realms of the spirit. Their delight in the beauty of his imagery and the lilt of his lines has given them a new appreciation of poetry at its best. Whether the rhythm is that of Poor Tired Tim dragging his feet, of the glittering silver of the moon's rays on the landscape at night, or the soundless glide of "someone" who came knocking in eerie and mysterious fashion, Walter de la Mare has reproduced it in his lines with beauty, music, and imagination.

Paul Hazard has expressed this function of literature perhaps better than anyone else when he speaks of "books that offer children an intuitive and direct way of knowledge, a simple beauty capable of being perceived immediately, arousing in their souls a vibration which will endure all their lives; . . . when, instead of pouring out so much material on a child's soul that it is crushed, they plant in it a seed that will develop from the inside."[69]

Soon Walter de la Mare was joined by Rose Fyleman, whose *Fairies and Chimneys* (1920) was popular at once with the girls, first, because it was musical and, second, because it depicted the delicate antics of the fairies. Elizabeth Madox Roberts, on the other hand, introduced in her *Under the Tree* (1922) much nature poetry about the things children knew and understood. And then who should appear on the scene but Christopher Robin himself in *When We Were Very Young* (1924)!

As a forerunner of many later attractive anthologies of verse, Louis Untermeyer's *This Singing World; An Anthology of Modern Poetry for Young People* first appeared in 1923. It introduced a wealth of new verse without discarding the best of the old. It was imaginatively conceived and organized under headings which immediately appealed to children: *Laughing Legends*, for example, *Rhyme without Reason, Open Roads,* and *Breath of the Earth.* Its delicately fanciful illustrations were well suited to the selections. In his introduction to the volume, Untermeyer said frankly to the children: "You won't like all of these poems. . . . There are in this remarkable world as many flavors as tastes."[70] Then he pointed out different poems suited to different tastes and guided young readers in finding individual selections which would bring them satisfaction. Helen Dean Fish's *The Boy's Book of Verse* (1923) advertised by its very title that there was not a daffodil or a dandelion in the lot! Walter de la Mare's *Come Hither* (1923) offered excellent poems from old standard verse for more mature and selective readers. Nearly fifty per cent of the book was devoted to background materials written by the poet "About and Roundabout" the poems.

Juvenile books between 1910 and 1925 began to look toward the children's own world. Elmer Boyd Smith produced his picture books on the farm, the seashore, railroads, and shipping.[71] In *Chicken World* (1910) especially, he showed his power to picture the details and colors of animals and farm life in illustrations which themselves carry the story apart from the text.

Realistic fiction. Real children became the subject of fiction in Clara W. Hunt's *About Harriet* (1916) and Dorothy Canfield's *Understood Betsy* (1917), the latter an early effort to reveal the true psychology of childhood. Charles P. Burton's *Boy Scouts of Bob's Hill* (1912), Joseph Gollomb's *That Year at Lincoln High* (1918), and William Heyliger's *High Benton* (1919) were initial attempts to present boy life as it is. Though later efforts proved more successful, this was at least a beginning in a very important area of fiction. Boys who had lived through the declaration of World War I were grateful for a good laugh in Booth Tarkington's *Penrod* (1914), which remained popular through several decades.

Children of other lands. In the revelation of children of other lands, this period was also one of transition. Lucy Fitch Perkins's famous *Twins* series flourished. Certain titles like *The Dutch Twins* (1911) and *The Eskimo Twins* (1914) made individual children and their homelands real to American boys and girls although a visit to Ellis Island was the author's nearest approach to the countries about which she wrote. Dikken Zwilgmeyer's stories, translated from the Norwegian by Emilie Poulsson added Inger Johanne *(What Happened to Inger Johanne as Told by Herself,* 1919) and Johnny Blossom *(Johnny Blossom,* 1912) to the world's children whose "lively doings" were very much alike in all nations. The difference between these first efforts and the spontaneous and animated children who peopled the book world in the thirties will be immediately apparent.

Hendrik Van Loon and others. A whole series of significant books of history revealed, between 1910 and 1925, the growing respect for children in offering them the best—both in manner of telling and in the accuracy of research backgrounds. In 1911 Eva March Tappan introduced a new approach to history in her ever popular *When Knights Were Bold.* It did not deal with battles and kings, but with modes of living in medieval times in castle and village, in manor houses and in monasteries; it traced the stages by which a squire became a knight and explained the influence of religion upon the lives of the people. *The Book of Discovery,* written in 1912 by Margaret Synge, revealed the romance and daring of the early explorers from the Phoenicians to the discovery of the South Pole, with copious quotes from diaries and use of woodcuts and old maps.

In the realm of straightforward factual accounts of history, the years from 1910 to

1925 showed notable advance in both number and quality. Battles were no longer the center of attention. Movements of people, ways of living, forces at work in the world—anthropological, geological, geographical, and scientific—were brought to bear upon the history of mankind. Hendrik W. Van Loon's *The Story of Mankind* (1921) won the Newbery Award in 1922. It changed the course of historical writing for years to come. After describing his wonder at the panoramic view of his own town which he had enjoyed on climbing to the top of its highest tower, he said to his sons, to whom the book was dedicated, "History is a mighty Tower of Experience which Time has built among the endless fields of bygone ages. It is no easy task to reach the top of this ancient structure to get the benefit of the full view. There is no elevator, but young feet are strong and it can be done."[72] It was this broad sweep of history with which his book dealt—with the geological changes of the earth, the ascent of man, the course of civilization, including patterns of social organization, the crafts men had developed, and the influence of machines on the course of the world's progress—all ending with a glimpse into the future.

Van Loon used old charts and maps, original sources, and tapestries to make the story real to children. Then he left his sons with the message, "The world is in dreadful need of men who will assume new leadership and who will recognize that we are only at the beginning of the voyage."[73]

Van Loon's *The Story of Mankind* was followed within three years by Virgil M. Hillyer's *A Child's History of the World* (1924). A teacher in the Calvert School in Baltimore, Mr. Hillyer complained that he had been brought up only on American history. "So far as I knew," he reported, "1492 was the beginning of the world. To me, Christ and His times belonged not to the realm of time and space, but to a spiritual realm."[74] This predicament he wanted to avoid for his children, so he told the story of the world's progress, not by nations but by periods, tracing movements, ideas, big events, and great names. His aim was to "take the child out of his self-centered life, to extend his horizon, broaden his view, and open up the vista down the ages past."[75] The history was revised in 1951 with the aid of Edward G. Huey.

Historical fiction. Historical fiction flourished at this time also. Cornelia Meigs's *Master Simon's Garden* (1916) became the forerunner of many distinguished volumes. In this story of three generations from Puritan days to the Revolution, "the garden and Master Simon stand serenely for color and gaiety against rigid Puritanism and intolerance."[76] Comparison of it with Elizabeth Speare's *The Witch of Blackbird Pond* (1958) shows what has happened to orient such fiction toward the interests and concerns of adolescence without destroying the vividness of the historical background. *Master Simon's Garden* was followed in the early twenties by Charles Boardman

Hawes's *The Mutineers* (1920) and *The Dark Frigate* (1923) and by Caroline Dale Snedeker's stories of ancient times like *The Perilous Seat* (1923) and *Theras and His Town* (1924).

More biography. Closely related to these narratives were the biographies of historic characters. Ida Tarbell's *The Boy Scouts' Life of Lincoln* (1921) was based upon a two-volume life of Lincoln for adults, for which she had gathered a wealth of sound data. Somewhat earlier Albert Bigelow Paine's intimately personal *The Boys' Life of Mark Twain* (1916) and Laura E. Richards's sprightly *Abigail Adams and Her Times* (1917) had appeared. Both were forerunners of an important area of biography yet to be developed, for neither of the subjects was a soldier, a sailor, or a president of the United States.

The effect of the motion picture and the national parks. Frederic G. Melcher, who was always close to booksellers' problems as well as to those of teachers and librarians, in reviewing in 1928 thirty years of children's books, discussed the salutary effect upon the writing and sale of books of the coming of the movie "as a purveyor of diversion and instruction" and of the radio, "a new invention by which the creative ideas of one mind can be carried to others. In the last decade (1910-1920), the climax of these new inventions," he said, "there has been the greatest growth the book has ever known!"[77] A part of the emphasis of these media was on Indians and westerns, stimulated also by the opening of Glacier and Rocky Mountain National Parks —hence the increasing popularity of Altsheler's stories and of such books as James W. Schultz's *With the Indians in the Rockies* (1911) and George Grinnell's tales of the Indians and the opening of the West. At the same time, Masefield added to adventure fiction *Jim Davis* (1912), a story filled with the mystery and suspense of smugglers on the Devon Coast. Two other popular tales of adventure with animals came out at this time, both combining plot interest with romanticized backgrounds—Eleanor Atkinson's *Greyfriars Bobby* (1912) and Olaf Baker's *Shasta of the Wolves* (1919).

The work of Caroline Hewins. The growing richness of the whole field of children's books is revealed in a remarkable book list (1915) addressed to parents and to librarians by Caroline M. Hewins under the auspices of the American Library Association. It indicates a trend toward more books for young children and less reliance on adult books for older ones. It lists the *Fifty-Must-Haves* and groups all books under topical headings such as travel, astronomy, home and school, fairy tales and wonder stories. It offers practical advice for interesting children in books and concludes with a remark still quoted frequently:

> No college English, no finishing-school course in art or literature will ever give men or women what they might have had if books had been as much their friends in childhood as the children next door.[78]

INFLUENCES AT WORK DURING
THE TRANSITION

The period from 1925 to 1940, to be discussed later, has been variously entitled the Golden Age of Children's Literature in America and the Volcanic Eruption in Books for Boys and Girls. Many factors contributed to the sudden increase in the production of more and better books. It may be well to look back at this point upon the factors at work between 1910 and 1925 which made such rapid progress possible. After the First World War there was an upsurge of hope that the world was now safe for democracy and that the time was ripe for attention to the things of the spirit.

The influence of Anne Carroll Moore. Moreover, there were leaders trained for the task and eager to push forward to the improvement of books for children. In 1906 Anne Carroll Moore had come from the Pratt Institute to be head of the Children's Room of the New York Public Library. Fired with a zeal to bring children only the best, she gathered around her a group of able women in the publishing world. She began the critical reviews of children's books which appeared in *The Bookman* in 1918. Not since the days when Horace E. Scudder in *The Riverside Magazine* and Thomas Bailey Aldrich in *The Atlantic Monthly* had inveighed against wooden characterization, sentimentalism, and didacticism in books for boys and girls, with characters their own age who "still wore heads out of all proportion to their shoulders,"[79] had chil-

dren's books enjoyed the privilege of adult attention.[80]

Then in 1924 in her weekly column in the *New York Herald Tribune: Books,* under the title *The Three Owls* (author, artist, and critic), Miss Moore began her campaign to make known the best and to discredit the inferior. The triumvirate was significant because it stood for cooperation among groups which had had little contact with one another before her day. She demanded the best for children—books distinguished in text and appropriate and artistic in illustration and format. Her critical standards were high. She constantly set before publisher, buyer, and reader the rigorous criteria by which she believed books should be judged. Of those which were to be offered to children she demanded originality, beauty, spontaneous appeal, and an imaginative rather than merely a realistic approach. Fortunately, many of these papers have been preserved in book form in such volumes as *My Roads to Childhood*, a compilation of essays from three previous books, published after her death by The Horn Book, Incorporated.[81]

Anne Carroll Moore made her library a meeting place for children and authors. She welcomed foreign writers and artists and introduced them to Americans in their chosen fields. "Her office," wrote James Daugherty, "was a dynamic center where sooner or later you encountered nearly every vital worker in the field of children's books come to discuss new ideas at this source of inspiration."[82] Poets gathered in her library to read their poems to the children, and artists brought their pictures to display there. "The Three Owls themselves flew around the world and back again, bringing the talents of artists, poets, historians, storytellers, and critics to the consideration of books for children, relating books and reading not only to the lives of children, but to the wider, richer main stream of American culture."[83]

The place of the children's book editors. But Miss Moore was not alone in her fight for good books for children. In 1919 Louise Seaman Bechtel became children's book editor of the Macmillan Company, heading the first juvenile book department in a major publishing house. In 1923 May Massee went in the same capacity to Doubleday and later to Viking, where her lively imagination and her clear concept of the unity of form and idea helped to win more Newbery and Caldecott awards for her authors than were awarded to those of any other publisher. "It was the imaginative and pioneering spirit of such editors," wrote James Daugherty, "in enlisting new and often untried talent that opened windows and **brought fresh air into the stuffy atmosphere** of children's book publishing of that day. It is perhaps needless to add that it is largely due to the taste, intelligence, and courage of such editing that the present high standard and quality of children's books have been achieved."[84]

The coming of the children's rooms in public libraries. Children's rooms in public libraries and the people in charge of them had become more and more active throughout the United States in the last years of the nineteenth century. By 1904 such rooms were in all Carnegie libraries in the country, dedicated to serve the child on playgrounds, in scouting and other organizations, in schools or wherever he might be found. There was a clear recognition of the public library as a community service, "an independent educational agency, coordinate with, rather than subsidiary to, the public schools."[85] Emphasis was to be on the individual reader and his voluntary use of books. He was to enjoy privacy of thought and to pursue his own interests in broad areas of reading as contrasted with the textbook assigned reading in the schools. Such leaders as Anne Carroll Moore, Louise Seaman Bechtel, Mary Gould Davis, Effie Power, and Jessie Van Cleve promoted this purpose with foresight and vigor. By 1956 between forty and forty-four per cent of the circulation of most public libraries came from the children's rooms.[86]

The growth of the school library. At the same time, it was obvious that if all children were to have the benefit of such services, they must be available also in the schools. In 1896 a school library section had been established in the National Education Association followed by active committee work in the next three decades to promote libraries in the schools. By 1915 a School Library Division was set up in the American Library Association. At its annual meeting in San Francisco in 1947, the National Association of School Librarians presented pioneer citations to those who had given special impetus to the movement in its early days. These were conferred upon Martha Caroline Pritchard for her early recognition of the importance of elementary school libraries and the need of special education for school librarians, to Lucille Fargo for the improvement of school library administration, to Martha Wilson for the development of state library services in state departments of education, to Mary E. Hall for her interpretation of school libraries to the American Library Association and to the National Education Association, and to Annie Spencer Cutter for bringing about cooperation between school and public libraries.[87]

The influence of the National Council of Teachers of English. The National Council of Teachers of English also lent its influence very early to the movement to upgrade children's reading and to fill the gap between college entrance requirements and the cheap series to which children and young people devoted themselves during their leisure hours. The first committee appointed by the Council was a committee on *Home Reading,* chaired by Dr. Arlo Bates in 1911.

Franklin T. Baker, the second president of the Council, prepared *A Bibliography of Children's Reading* in 1906 at the request of teachers and librarians for a fuller guide to children's books, which would include a wider range of topics for supplementary reading than were then available.

"Books of information," he said, "though commonly treated with contempt by those who praise 'mere literature,' are nonetheless interesting and valuable to young readers, and are therefore included. Stories of children's lives, if told with life and spirit, have also been admitted. The standards of choice have been, the author ventures to believe, rather liberal and catholic than the reverse. He hopes, however, that they have not been so liberal as to make his list an unsafe guide."[88] Dr. Baker paid tribute to "the tenderness toward childhood" of writers in the second half of the nineteenth century, but deplored "their imperfect understanding of what childhood is" and "their consequent inability to identify with children."[89] He made a plea for the child's right to be entertained as well as to be instructed and begged writers to remember that children's interest is in the life of action rather than in the life of thought. "Boys are not scholars," he said, "and most of them are not even scholars in the making. But they are men in the making, and good ideals are an exceedingly valuable element in the process."[90]

Some books, Dr. Baker admitted, gave him more trouble than all the rest. They were the so-called "girls" books. "They are numerous," he said, "and they are often painfully weak, and they seem to have been written mostly by people deficient in good red blood. They lack invention, action, humor; they run on (or off) in a patter of endless talk without point and without savor. Of course, they are not all bad. Louisa Alcott is almost, if not quite, a classic. And she has some worthy successors. But the tradition seems still to hold [1909] that anything will do for girls, if only there isn't too much in it."[91]

Perhaps the most interesting observation in Dr. Baker's discussion is that there were "too many books" appearing for children, and that the problem had become one not of *discovery* but of *discrimination*. One wonders what his verdict would be today!

In the second decade of the century, James F. Hosic, first executive secretary of the Council and later its president, toured the country in behalf of a course in Children's Literature for all prospective elementary school teachers and urged the creation of libraries "in the grades."[92] Today 73 per cent of all institutions preparing teachers for elementary schools require such a course.[93] The National Council of Teachers of English in 1963 recommended that it be a required part of the preparation of all elementary teachers.[94] Evidence also indicates that one-third of all elementary schools in this country have libraries.[95] There is still room for improvement. As chairman of the National Committee on the Reorganization of English in Secondary Schools in 1917, Dr. Hosic urged that literature be taught in such a way as "to lead to eager and appreciative reading of books of as high an order as is possible for the given individual to the end of both present and future development of his character and the formation of the habit of turning to good books for companionship in hours of leisure. To this purpose," he said, "all other purposes must be secondary."[96]

The Child Study Association of America. The Children's Book Committee of the Child Study Association of America began its reviews of children's books of the year as early as 1909. The results of the deliberations of twenty-five persons, including parents, librarians, educators, writers, anthologists, and booksellers appear in its annual publication, *Books of the Year,* a selection of some three hundred or more titles, grouped by ages and topics, and carefully annotated to guide parents and others in the selection of books for children.[97]

The Boy Scouts, the Children's Book Council, and National Children's Book Week. Mention has already been made of the establishment of the first National Children's Book Week in 1919 at the instigation of Franklin K. Mathiews, librarian of the Boy Scouts of America. Appalled by the low standards of reading he found on a visit to Boy Scout troups throughout the country, he persuaded Frederic G. Melcher, then executive secretary of the American Booksellers' Association, to inaugurate at the annual convention of that organization in Boston a National Children's Book Week. The growing number of cities, schools, and libraries that now unite annually in this celebration shows that it has met a very real need.

Today, Book Week is sponsored by the

Children's Book Council of some sixty children's editors, the first of whom were appointed by Macmillan and Doubleday more than forty years ago. They plan and distribute annually materials useful for the celebration.[98]

Frederic G. Melcher and the Newbery Medal. In June, 1922, Mr. Melcher created the Newbery Medal to give recognition annually to the children's book selected by a committee of librarians as the most distinguished contribution of the year to American literature for children. The award is announced in March of each year from Mr. Melcher's office and is presented at the annual dinner of the Children's Library Association in the summer. At this time an acceptance paper is read by the author and a sketch of his life and work is given by someone closely associated with him. These papers are published in *The Horn Book Magazine.* "The establishing of the Newbery Award," said Bertha Mahony Miller in the introduction to *Newbery Medal Books: 1922-1955,* "has had an incalculably stimulating effect not only upon authors, artists, and publishers, but also upon the public interest in children's books." It has likewise "stimulated the gradual development of critical judgment among librarians, teachers, and parents" and has "helped to sustain book interest throughout the year."[99]

Periodicals about children's books. In 1924 came the initiation of two periodicals concerned with children's books—*The Horn Book Magazine* of the Boston Bookshop for Boys and Girls established by the Women's Educational Union and *The Elementary English Review* edited by C. C. Certain of Detroit. The latter ultimately became the organ of the elementary school section of the National Council of Teachers of English. Under the able leadership of Bertha Mahony, of Jennie Lindquist, and now of Ruth Hill Viguers, *The Horn Book Magazine* has become far more than the organ of the Women's Educational Union. At the modest price of fifty cents for four issues per year, it made its first announcement of purpose: "We blow our horns for the best in Children's Literature, for books beautifully written and finely illustrated. . . . Our jovial huntsmen shall lead children over the hills and far away to the magic land of storybooks, where twentieth century boys and girls may follow and adventure."[100]

Today *The Horn Book Magazine,* which is probably the major source of high critical standards for the selection of children's books in the United States, appears monthly. With a personal touch not achieved by any other journals, it brings authors, illustrators, librarians, and teachers together through mutual respect for and genuine interest in books for boys and girls. Personal articles by authors and illustrators about their own work, informative articles about the lives and personalities of men and women of the children's book world, discussion of standards of selection of books of various kinds, and monthly reviews of acceptable books which culminate in an annual selection of the Fanfare Books of each year make *The Horn Book Magazine* indispensable for both teachers and librarians throughout the country.[101]

The Elementary English Review, known since 1947 as *Elementary English,* has through the years served varying needs of teachers of the language arts in the elementary school. As a service enterprise for the schools, it is concerned with a wide range of ability among youthful readers and with practical classroom plans for bringing books and boys and girls together. One of its chief purposes is to help teachers and librarians meet all of the reading needs of literally all of the children in the community and to relate reading to every aspect of the curriculum. Its lead article usually introduces an important writer for children. Each issue reviews recent books in terms of their value for both the individual and the curriculum.[102]

Most issues of *The Elementary English Review* opened with articles by or about well-known children's writers and illustrators. "Dr. Dolittle, the Children, and the Droll 'Huge' Lofting" was a favorite article in the first year of the publication.[103] Padraic Colum, Charles Boardman Hawes, and Charles J. Finger followed in later issues. Book Week activities encouraged teachers to make use of the stimulation which came from the new celebration. Helen Mackintosh presented her early research in children's choices of poetry,[104] and Wilma L. Garnett, hers on children's choices of prose.[105] Hugh Lofting and Clara W. Hunt

prepared book lists for developing world friendship through children's books, and Martha Caroline Pritchard described the beginnings of an elementary school library, complete with the list of titles included.[106] A year later C. C. Certain himself, as chairman of a joint committee on elementary school library standards of the National Education Association and the American Library Association, defined the elementary school library "in dollars and cents."[107] Book lists for Christmas and for vacation reading helped the teacher to stimulate young readers to make good use of their free time.

Changes in education influencing the use of books. Other changes were developing rapidly in the schools. Problem solving and thinking were being substituted for mere rote learning. Children were thrown on their own resources to find materials in books. Many interrelationships among subjects of study were explored. The Winnetka Plan (1913-1932) and the Dalton Plan (1920-26) required much more independent reading than had been customary.[108] After World War I an emphasis upon moral responsibility and upon worthy use of leisure came to the fore in the elementary school, and international understanding became a major objective of the program. In all this enrichment of the curriculum, the use of books and libraries received special emphasis. Books had to be furnished on a wider range of topics than before and on many levels of difficulty. Research had proved that the longer children of different levels of ability remain in school, the greater will be the differences in achievement among them.[109]

At this time also came the two children's encyclopedias—*The World Book Encyclopedia* in 1917 and *Compton's Pictured Encyclopedia* in 1922. Both were the work of distinguished scholars, specialists in the field in which they were writing, and yet both were written in a way to stimulate and interest children.

A Fourth Owl in children's book selection. C. C. Certain exerted a powerful influence on behalf of the availability of books for wide reading in the schools. He had a hard-headed interest in basing conclusions on the evidence of research. He mistrusted adults who determined reading standards for today's children on recollections of their own childhood reading of twenty-five to fifty years before. He knew that all of the children of all of the people were in the schools, that some of them could read and some of them could not. He wanted to know the facts about the habits of reading of everybody's children. He therefore published in *The Elementary English Review* the results of surveys of reading interests in the schools. Before 1930, a Fourth Owl had joined the three already established by Miss Moore— and that was the child himself. Dr. Certain studied the evidence of the new reading tests as to the extent of individual differences in ability to read and the nature of individual interests in the selection of books. He constantly faced the facts squarely, urg-

ing a search for better books to satisfy the normal interests of children and a wider variety of them to meet realistically the varied levels of ability found in the average school room.

The struggle between realism and fairy lore. In all this turmoil, differences of opinion between and among librarians and teachers were widespread. In 1920 there appeared in *The Bookman* a list of books suitable for Christmas gifts for children from two to ten.[110] Only three of the books recommended presented to the child the life around him. All the rest were highly imaginative and belonged to the folk or fairy tale world. Two of the three were books of poetry— Robert Louis Stevenson's *A Child's Garden of Verses* (1885) and Ralph W. Bergengren's *Jane, Joseph, and John* (1918). The other was Elmer Boyd Smith's *Chicken World* (1910), an attractive picture book with a farm setting. But what of the changing world these children had to face? What of their lively curiosity concerning the things around them? In 1921 Lucy Sprague Mitchell, whose studies in philosophy and psychology had led to a new concept of what lies behind the interests of childhood, brought out her *Here and Now Story Book* for children from two to seven.[111]

"I have assumed," she said in the introduction, "that anything to which a child gives his spontaneous attention, anything which he questions as he moves around the world, holds appropriate material about which to talk to him either in speech or in writing. I have assumed that answers to these inquiries should be given always in terms of a relationship which is natural and intelligible at his age and which will help him to order the familiar facts of his own experiences.[112]

Hence, her stories, which are told in motor and sensory terms and in the rhythms of the young child's own speech, include for the two-year-old such simple stories as "Marnie Gets Dressed in the Morning"; for the five-year-old, "How the Singing Water Got into the Tub"; and for the seven-year-old, "Boris Takes a Walk and Finds Many Different Kinds of Trains." Another *Here and Now Story Book* appeared in 1937,[113] and a new and enlarged edition in 1948.[114] As the child's environment had changed greatly in the twenty-seven years since the appearance of the first volume, the stories had also been altered in theme and character. In the last edition, Mrs. Mitchell repeated her earlier charge:

> It is only the blind eye of the adult that finds the familiar uninteresting. The attempt to amuse children by presenting them with the strange, the bizarre, the unreal, is the unhappy result of adult blindness. Children do not find the unusual piquant until they are firmly acquainted with the usual; they do not find the preposterous humorous until they have intimate knowledge of ordinary behavior; they do not get the point of alien environments until they are securely oriented in their own. Too often we mistake excitement for genuine interest and give the children stimulus instead of food. The fairy story,

the circus, the novelty-hunting delight the sophisticated adult; they excite and confuse the child. Red Riding Hood and the circus Indians excite the little child. Cinderella confuses him. Not one clarifies any relationship which will further his efforts to order the world.[115]

Not all the fairy tales were taboo. Simple stories like *The Three Bears* and *The Bremen Town Musicians* were included in the program.

The answer came back immediately that loss of vision is never compensated for by gain of sight. Fortunately, the intervening years have brought to children many beautifully designed books for the interpretation of their own environment and a more careful selection of fairy tales suited to their level of development.

The argument, however, has persisted. Perhaps two quotes, one from a psychologist and one from a man of letters, will reveal the nature of the conflict: Harry Overstreet, as late as 1929, presented his views of the case against the fairy tale:

> People have the curious notion that fairy tales build up the imaginative life of children. As a matter of fact, they pervert the imaginative life. Fairy tales are a left-over from primitive "science." The savage had no notion or only the vaguest notion of cause and effect. His world was largely one of magic. Things happened by miracle. A presto, an open sesame, and the trick was turned. It has taken the world countless thousands of weary years to get beyond that primitive state of mind. Most of the degrading misconceptions that man has had about his life here and hereafter,

arose out of his inability to detect cause and effect.

And now parents insist on inflicting this primitivism, this pathetic infantilism of the race on their children, forcing them to think uncausally, magically, miraculously, forcing them to habituate themselves to the technique of dreamy wishfulfillment rather than guiding them to the noble technique of observation, exploration, experiment, and objective achievement.

There are more things under heaven and on earth than are dreamed of in any of the fairy tales. The real world is a marvel as fascinating to the child as to the adult. Introduce the child vividly, interestingly, to that world, and we stir his imagination into life—his real imagination, not that sorry substitute for imagination which cowers in terror of witches and werewolves or gloats with triumphant joy over riches and power achieved without effort.[116]

Hamilton Wright Mabie, a well-known editor and journalist of his day, has expressed the opposite point of view in his introduction to *Fairy Tales Every Child Should Know:*

The fairy tale is a poetic recording of the facts of life, an interpretation by the imagination of its hard conditions, an effort to reconcile the spirit which loves freedom and goodness and beauty with its harsh, bare, and disappointing conditions . . . .

The faculty which created the fairy tale is the same faculty which, supplemented by a broader observation and based on more accurate knowledge, has broadened the range and activities of modern man, made the world accessible to him, enabled him to live in one place, but to speak and act in places thousands of miles distant, given him command of colossal forces, and is fast making him rich on a scale which would have seemed incredible to men of a half-century ago. There is nothing in any fairy tale more marvelous and inherently improbable than many of the achievements of scientific observation and invention, and we are only at the beginning of the wonders that lie within the reach of the human spirit. . . .

No one can understand the modern world without the aid of the imagination, and as the frontiers of knowledge are pushed still further away from the obvious and familiar, there will be an increasing tax on the imagination. The world of dead matter which our fathers thought they understood has become a world of subtle forces moving with inconceivable velocity; nothing is inert; all things are transformed into other and more elusive shapes precisely as the makers of the fairy tales foresaw and predicted; the world lives in every atom just as their world lived; forces lie just outside the range of physical sight, but entirely within the range of spiritual vision, precisely as the tellers of these old stories divined. Mystery and wonder enfold all things, and not only evoke the full play of the mind, but flood it with intimations and suggestions of the presence of more elusive and subtle forces, of finer and more obedient powers, as the world of fairies, magi, and demons enfolded the ancient earth of daily toil and danger.

In a word, the fairy stories have come true; they are historical in the sense that they faithfully report a stage of spiritual growth and predict a higher order of realities through a deeper knowledge of actualities. They were poetic renderings of the facts which science is fast verifying, chiefly by the use of the same faculty which enriched early literature with the myth and the fairy tale. The scientist has turned poet in these later days, and the imagination which once expressed itself in a free handling of facts so as to make them answer the needs and demands of the human spirit, now expresses itself in that breadth of vision which reconstructs an extinct animal from a bone and analyzes the light of a sun flaming on the outermost boundaries of space.[117]

An entertaining corollary to this is Elizabeth Enright's recent plea for more stories about the everyday world of boys and girls:

> We have lost our taste for magic because we have, in many cases, made it come true. Voices do speak out of the air. There *is* a wonderbox that shows us visions. Our version of the magic carpet travels across every sky carrying its load of commercial travelers, elderly relatives, or bags of mail; and if the cow has not yet jumped over the moon, the little dog who laughed to see such sport has already encircled the earth a great number of times. As for the dragons, they are positively commonplace;

they stutter and racket in the farmer's fields, hoot through every city street, and bellow their fire across the battlefields. Dragons are everywhere.[118]

It is interesting to look back upon the same controversy as it had developed more than a century ago. Writing of Maria Edgeworth, Florence Barry said: "If she never understood the fairy Way of Writing, it was because she had built a school upon the fairy circles of her village green. Her children were so happy that they never discovered an enchanted wood. They planted trees instead of climbing them; they knew all the roads to Market, but nobody showed them the way to Fairyland.[119] Fortunately, the result of the controversy today is that there is room in the realm of children's books for both the schoolhouse and the fairy circles, and the village green and the enchanted wood are making complementary contributions to the children's reading world.

The Golden Age of Children's Books—1925-1940

By 1925 the children's book world was ready for its Golden Age. As has been said, there had been an upsurge of hope after World War I that the world was now safe for democracy and there was time for the

things of the spirit. For more than twenty years, teachers and librarians had been setting the stage for a revival of interest in children's books. At least two periodicals were channeling to parents, teachers, and librarians good news about better books for boys and girls.

THE NEW PRINTING PROCESSES

New offset processes of printing had been invented. They had been brought from Europe after World War I and reproduced in our own country. Before this time, the colorful pictures of Maxfield Parrish and Edmund Dulac and the delicate imaginative drawings of Arthur Rackham had been inserts in the books which they adorned. From now on, with the new offset printing, the pictures could be more than decorative; they could join the text in telling the story.

THE INFLUX OF FOREIGN ARTISTS AND AUTHORS

Finally, numbers of foreign artists and authors had come to the United States after the war, seeking a new freedom in artistic expression. Thanks to Anne Carroll Moore and her associates, they found here an atmosphere of enthusiasm and of high purpose and an appreciation of what they had to offer. Here was a ferment about children's books to which they themselves contributed significantly.

Padraic Colum from Ireland was among the first to arrive to join forces with the Hungarian artist, Willy Pogany, in recreating for American and British children the significant stories of Greek legendary lore. Miska Petersham came from Hungary to illustrate, with his American wife, Margery Clark's *The Poppy Seed Cakes* (1924) and ultimately to set forth for their own son the gay journey of Miki (*Miki,* 1929) with the Hungarian gypsies.

The Petershams were followed by the Aulaires, Edgar from Switzerland and Ingri from Norway, who, after study in Paris, did their *Ola* (1932) for American boys and girls, followed by *Children of the Northlights* in 1935. Here was a new kind of printing with artistically shaded colors lithographed from plates cut in stone. Then came Kurt Wiese from Germany via China to illustrate Marjorie Flack's *The Story about Ping* (1933) and Phil Stong's *Honk: the Moose* (1935), revealing the skill in drawing the humorous and personable creatures for which he was to become famous in books of his own.

By 1935 Kate Seredy, who was here from Hungary, was persuaded by May Massee to reproduce something of the life of her own country in *The Good Master.* Two years later, she won the Newbery Award for her spirited and imaginative interpretation of the aspiration of her own people in *The White Stag* (1937). May Massee herself, who lived through these exciting days with the newcomers, has described the experience vividly:

> The pressures of afterwar and prewar and war years brought many artists who loved the countries of their youth that had been left behind and who, perhaps from nostalgia that gave them a long perspective, could make better books for children here than if they had stayed at home. Here they found means to express themselves, and in this period produced hundreds of picture

books and stories vividly proving that though scenes and customs vary, children are the same the world over, that there is beauty and goodness everywhere. And there were second- and third-generation artists—Americans—who in their growing up had absorbed some of the cultures of their forebears, and so consciously and unconsciously could enrich the pattern of American life that they were presenting to their children. The children's rooms welcomed them all, encouraging books as they appeared, and so inspiring more to come. All in all, by midcentury it is safe to say that American children's literature was the most cosmopolitan literature in the world.[120]

From *The White Stag* by Kate Seredy. Il. by author. Viking, 1937.

THE MAKING OF THE AMERICAN PICTURE BOOK

What happened in the realm of native American picture books can best be illustrated by calling the roll of some of the most distinguished among them which appeared during the Golden Age.

In 1927 William Nicholson produced *Clever Bill*, probably the first picture story book published in America although written and illustrated in England. Its pictures carry the story of the little red-coated soldier who refused to be left behind when his mistress forgot to take him with her on her journey. Wanda Ga'g, born, as she said, in a little Old World German community called New Ulm, Minnesota, produced in 1928 her exquisite *Millions of Cats* done in the spirit

From *Millions of Cats* by Wanda Ga'g. Il. by author. Coward, 1928.

of German folklore. In 1930, Elizabeth Coatsworth brought out her *The Cat Who Went to Heaven,* a reverent story with a Japanese flavor and striking animal pictures by Lynd Ward.

In 1930 and 1931 came Marjorie Flack's *Angus*, first with the ducks (*Angus and the Ducks,* 1930) and then with the cat (*Angus*

From *The Story of Ferdinand* by Munro Leaf and Robert Lawson.
Il. by Robert Lawson. Viking, 1936.

and the Cat, 1931), to be a universal favorite among little children. Munro Leaf and Robert Lawson's *The Story of Ferdinand* (1936) brought a laugh to readers of all ages. During the same year Clare T. New-

From *Little Tim and the Brave Sea Captain* by Edward Ardizzone.
Il. by author. Walck, 1955.

berry began her inimitable drawings of kittens in her picture book called *Mittens* (1936), and Edward Ardizzone from England appeared with *Little Tim and the Brave Sea Captain,* the dramatic tale of Little Tim's first voyage on the rolling deep (1936).

In 1937 Dr. Seuss produced what is perhaps his best picture book, *And to Think That I Saw It on Mulberry Street,* distinguished for its extravagant nonsense and its truth to the experience of imaginative children everywhere. The next year (1938) brought three distinguished picture books: James Daugherty's *Andy and the Lion,* with

From *Andy and the Lion* by James Daugherty.
Il. by author. Viking, 1938.

its display of muscles which the author was destined later to use in very different settings; Thomas Handforth's *Mei Li,* with its pictures as vigorous and as attractive as the little Chinese girl herself; and Claire Huchet Bishop's *The Five Chinese Brothers,* which brought a favorite Oriental folk tale to

From *Mei Li* by Thomas Handforth.
Il. by author. Doubleday, 1938.

American children with never-to-be-forgotten drawings by Kurt Wiese. Ludwig Bemelmans's *Madeline,* appearing in 1939, introduced an inimitably French setting and a little girl whom children took to their hearts at once.

With *Little Toot* (1939), Hardie Gramatky introduced an animated tugboat which, through the author's humanized drawings, became as clear a personality to young readers as any child of picture book fame. Small wonder that Anne Carroll Moore insisted on coupling its appearance with the christening of one of New York's tugboats with Christopher Morley as master of ceremonies! Along with Mary Liddell's earlier

From *Little Toot* by Hardie Gramatky.
Il. by author. Putnam, 1939.

Little Machinery, which had appeared in 1926, and Virginia Lee Burton's *Mike Mulligan and His Steam Shovel* (1939), *Little Toot* led a whole procession of animated trains, boats, automobiles, and machines which were to follow in the next decade.

In variety of themes, in originality of concept, and in the use of both color and black and white, this era of picture books enriched the field of children's literature perhaps more than any other single period in its history and set a standard for years to come.

Three of the best picture books of the thirties were religious in theme. The Petershams' *The Christ Child* (1931) is a reverent, inspirational picture book, illustrating the story of the birth of Jesus from the King James Version of the Bible with quietly joyous pictures in blue and yellow and rose. Helen Sewell's *A First Bible* (1934) with full-page illustrations of favorite Old Testament characters reveals the sense of thoughtfulness, dignity, and peace which she so frequently achieves through an artistic use of light and shade. Dorothy Lathrop's *Animals of the Bible,* with text supplied by Helen Dean Fish (1937), revealed her special talent for drawing silky, furry creatures and her sincere feeling for the Biblical verses she was illustrating.

THE COMING OF THE CALDECOTT MEDAL

The advent of the Caldecott Medal, established by Frederic G. Melcher in 1938 for the best picture book of the year, helped to center still further attention upon the qualities which differentiate a distinguished picture book from other notable books for children.[121] *Animals of the Bible* (1937), the first winner of the award, demonstrated them admirably.

EXPERIMENTS WITH PHOTOGRAPHIC PICTURE BOOKS

Realizing that this was the period of the depression, one wonders that so much could

From *A First Bible* by Helen Sewell. Il. by author. Walck, 1934.

have been accomplished. Many publishers at this time began experimenting with less expensive books. Mary S. Martin and Edward Steichen brought out in 1930 their *The First Picture Book* with simple, clear photographs of objects in a baby's environment. It was a book for the "pointing stage" which May Lamberton Becker described so understandingly in her *First Adventures in Reading.*[122] *The First Picture Book* was followed in 1931 by Lena Towsley's *Peggy and Peter; What They Did Today*. The daily doings of these two children were illustrated by attractive photographs.

THE IMAGINATIVE STORY

In the realm of the imaginative story, Wallace Wadsworth introduced his obstreperous *Paul Bunyan and His Great Blue Ox* (1926). Christopher Robin was joined by the redoubtable Pooh in *Winnie-the-Pooh* (1926)

From *Winnie-the-Pooh* by A. A. Milne. Il. by Ernest H. Shepard. Dutton, 1926.

and in *The House at Pooh Corner* (1928). Elizabeth MacKinstry did her highly imaginative and colorful pictures for the Comtesse D'Aulnoy's *The White Cat and Other Old French Fairy Tales* (1928), and Wanda Ga'g produced her *Snow White and the Seven Dwarfs* (1938) in rhythmical and diminutive German fashion to offset the effects of Walt Disney. This perfect little miniature may have set the fashion for illustrated editions of single fairy tales which have been done periodically ever since.

Fancy flourished during the thirties. The decade was introduced propitiously with Rachel Field's inimitable *Hitty, Her First Hundred Years* (1929), the story of the im-

perturbable New England doll, carved out of mountain-ash, who sat down in the antique shop, smiling and content, to write the memoirs of her first hundred years. She had survived philosophically a flight in a crow's beak to his nest in the top of a pine tree, shipwreck at sea in a burning whaler, worship as an idol by the heathen on a coconut island, life in a missionary family in Bombay, and attendance at a concert in the opera house in Philadelphia given by the

From *Hitty* by Rachel Field. Il. by Dorothy P. Lathrop. Macmillan, 1929.

prima donna, Adelina Patti. Like Hitty, the doll family in Anne Parrish's *Floating Island* (1930), to the great delight of little girls, carried on with equanimity and resourcefulness after surviving shipwreck. Then Mary Poppins (*Mary Poppins*, 1934) blew in on the east wind with all the eccentricities a youthful reader could demand. In 1937, Pecos Bill, "the greatest cowboy of all time," arrived from the West in James Bowman's robust story (*Pecos Bill*), which was followed in 1938 by Paul Leyssac's distinguished translation of Andersen's fairy tales called *It's Perfectly True and Other Stories*. Finally in 1939, Robert Lawson produced delicately imaginative illustrations for John Bunyan's *Pilgrim's Progress* as retold by Mary Godolphin in 1884.

AMERICAN CHILDREN IN BOOKS

By the thirties, stories of real boys and girls began to appear on the horizon, many of them representing the children who make up America. Laura Armer, out of her experience with the Indians of the Southwest, chose Waterless Mountain for the setting of her story of an Indian boy who grew up to be a medicine man. The distinguished pictures "in delicate, bright colors leave an impression in the mind of a rainbow shining in a tender, rain-washed sky."[123] The author's reverent treatment of the whole experience won for *Waterless Mountain* (1931) the Newbery Award in 1932. Ellis Credle's

Down, Down the Mountain (1934) made youngsters of the Blue Ridge Mountains very real to American boys and girls. Carol Ryrie Brink's Caddie Woodlawn (*Caddie Woodlawn*, 1935), although she grew up in pioneer days in Wisconsin, is not only herself but also every girl whose ambition is to be anything except a lady. As a period piece, however, it is without equal.

Mabel Leigh Hunt's impetuous little Quaker girl, embarrassed by her seven names, comes alive in the story, *The Little Girl with Seven Names* (1936). Finally after the neighbor's new baby proves to be a boy, she gives two of the names, Miranda and Amanda, to her twin baby sisters and has Melissa-Louisa-Cynthia-Jane-Farlow left. This is a warm family story. In *Henner's Lydia* (1936) Marguerite de Angeli reveals life in the Mennonite region of Pennsylvania. Ruth Sawyer's picture of Lucinda, roller skating on the sidewalks of lower New York (*Roller Skates*, 1936), is in direct contrast to that of Arna Bontemps's *Sad-Faced Boy* (1937) in Harlem. Next, Mabel Robinson wrote in *Bright Island* (1937) of the child of Maine whom she knew well.

Carolyn Haywood's *"B" Is for Betsy* (1939), the popular first book of a popular series, is set in the first grade—anywhere in the United States. The children's circus performance is a masterpiece. Two little boys playing elephant under a big gray covering get their legs entangled, and the elephant collapses on the floor. Only a person who has played circus in the first grade could have described the scene so realistically.

These are all books of distinction which reveal American boys and girls to each other, each treated with respect and endowed with individuality by the author.

CHILDREN AROUND THE WORLD

Periodically, in the field of children's books, there is a deluge of titles on a particular topic, especially if the publisher thinks they will sell to the schools. After the First World War, thoughtful Americans were exceedingly concerned about international understanding. Many cheap, ephemeral books for children came from the press monthly purporting to acquaint children with boys and girls around the world. Robert Lawson, looking back in 1940, remarked that "for a couple of seasons we had a flood of *Little Pedro and His Donkey in Mexico; Little Kookoo, the Eskimo, and His Pet Narwhal; Little Kong of Hong Kong and His Pet Duck;* and so forth until every children's book list read like morning roll call at Ellis Island."[124] Thus he pointed up the danger of filling library shelves with cheap, insincere books produced en masse for the sake of sales. In the realm of international understanding, certain books survived this period because the authors were sincere, they had intimate knowledge of the countries they described, and they wrote of

characters who were individuals and not merely types.

The 1930's saw the arrival of Elizabeth Morrow's *The Painted Pig* (1930), which revealed in brilliantly colorful pictures two Mexican children and their toys. It proved

From *The Painted Pig* by Elizabeth Morrow.
Il. by René d'Harnoncourt. Knopf, 1930.

to the children's book world how adequately a picture book could introduce the children of the world to one another, particularly with the help of a local artist like René d' Harnoncourt.

Among the most lovable of the children presented during this decade is Eleanor Lattimore's mischievous Little Pear (*Little Pear*, 1931), the lively youngest member of a closely knit Chinese family living along the river wharves of China, which offered ample stimulation for the activities of the hero of the story. Arthur Ransome's *Swallows and Amazons* (1931) reports the holiday adventures of two families of very real and ingenious children camping on an island in the English Lakes with two sail boats, "sharks" which are really pike, and an uncle who passes for a pirate. In 1934 Ludwig Bemelmans gave to little children his *Hansi*, the warm story of his own recollections of Christmas in his uncle's home high up in the Austrian Tyrol. The lively colors and dramatic winter scenes do justice even to the beauties of that spectacular region.

Kate Seredy's *The Good Master* (1935) is also based on recollections of a childhood visit to an uncle's farm in Hungary. The lively adventures of Kate and her cousin on horseback and in the traditional festivals of an old land combine with a staunch family feeling and an understanding of childhood to make this a distinguished story. The picturesque southwest coast of Ireland forms the background for Hilda Van Stockum's *The Cottage at Bantry Bay* (1938), the gentle story of family security and a background of Irish legendary lore.

When Robert Frost was asked by a reporter why he had written so little about Florida although he had been there often, he replied, "Poetry comes from where you get the dirt

From *The Good Master* by Kate Seredy. Il. by author. Viking, 1935.

in your fingers. Where you live and have your troubles. That's where your poetry comes from."[125] Every one of these writers, metaphorically speaking, has had his fingers in the soil of the country about which he writes. His books, therefore, are worthy of respect.

AMERICAN BACKGROUNDS IN FICTION

During the same period there were writers revealing American backgrounds whose fingers had also been in our soil. One of these was Carol Ryrie Brink, whose *Caddie Woodlawn* (1935) has already been mentioned in another connection. As a picture of life in pioneer days in Wisconsin, it is an authentic bit of Americana. Cornelia Meigs's *Willow Whistle* (1931) is another of the same calibre, and so is Elizabeth Coatsworth's *Away Goes Sally* (1934), the story of a pioneer child's exciting journey through New England in her own house drawn on a sledge by six yoke of oxen. But the person who stands out above all others in presenting pioneer life to children during the thirties is Laura Ingalls Wilder. The *Little House* series (1932-1943), opening up to young readers the sense of warm family relationships and the values of life represented in the crude cabin of pioneer days, somehow grips them and makes them ask for more. Girls are glad that *Little House in the Big Woods* (1932), *Little House on the Prairie* (1935), *These Happy Golden Years* (1943), and five other pioneer stories won recognition for their author in the establishment of the Laura Ingalls Wilder Award by the children's librarians of the American Library Association in 1954 to be given "to an author or illustrator whose books, published in the United States, have over a period of years made a substantial and lasting contribution to literature for children."[126] In honor of the occasion, a 1953 edition of the whole series was brought out by Harper with illustrations by Garth Williams.

ANIMAL STORIES AND MORE

A number of distinguished animal stories came out during this period, all of them deeply sensitive and all with settings which played an important part in the story. Will James's *Smoky, the Cowhorse* (1926) came straight from the range and the corral. As much at home with the roundup and the rodeo as he was with the picturesque cowboy speech in which his story is written, James described the life of a young, smoke-colored pony from his first encounter with coyotes, rattlesnakes, and cougars to his taming for the rodeo and his fight to free himself from the cruel half-breed. In the end, he was reunited with Clint, the only master he had ever acknowledged. Dhan Gopal Mukerji's *Kari the Elephant* (1922) and *Gay-Neck* (1927) are set in India. *Kari* gives an objective picture of a boy and his pet elephant in an authentic Indian setting. *Gay-Neck*, however, is concerned with the conflict between the Hindu religion and acts of war, so that much of the story is deeply philosophical in nature. The flight of the pigeon among war planes and his mission as a carrier involve war and fighting with alternate retreats to a monastery to get rid of the enmity in his soul. The striking drawings by Boris Artzybasheff helped win the book the Newbery Award. Only superior readers will read it for themselves, but many other children will enjoy hearing it read aloud.

Felix Salten's delicately beautiful deer story called *Bambi* (1928) with its sensitive revelation of the fears of the forest creatures has remained a classic through the years. Marjorie Kinnan Rawlings's *The Yearling* (1938) reveals suffering—the anguish of the boy who must do away with his pet yearling because it is destroying the meager crops of the family farm. Jody Baxter grows up in the process. Again, the story is introspective and depicts a peculiarly destitute and closely knit family in the Florida Cross Creek country. It, too, will be read primarily by gifted readers.

THE NEW POETRY

Poetry for children wore a rich new garb during the years from 1920 to 1940. In the first place, it looked enticing whether in the small, attractive books of selections from individual poets or in the gaily decorated and appealingly arranged anthologies. Rachel Field described both city and country in her *Taxis and Toadstools* (1926), a book of verses dealing primarily with familiar scenes. Among the special favorites of these years were A. A. Milne's *When We Were Very Young* (1924) and *Now We Are Six* (1927), both of which enchanted children from the moment they appeared.

Publishers brought out small, attractive editions of the poems of individual poets, which had special appeal for children. Vachel Lindsay's *Johnny Appleseed and Other Poems* (1928), *Edna St. Vincent Mil-* *lay's Poems Selected for Young People* (1929), Carl Sandburg's *Early Moon* (1930), Sara Teasdale's *Stars To-Night* (1930), and Emily Dickinson's *Poems for Youth* (1934) all appeared in beautiful format with sketches and attractive captions to entice young people to read. Rosemary and Stephen Vincent Benét's *A Book of Americans* (1933) gave boys and girls a good laugh in its characterizations of many notable persons in American history.

Blanche Thompson's *Silver Pennies* (1925) related distinctly modern poetry to the imaginative and everyday experiences of boys and girls in an attractive little volume which the youngest could hold with ease. Joseph Auslander and Frank E. Hill, in *The Winged Horse* (1927) and its accompanying anthology (1929), furnished a guide to English poetry for gifted readers. In 1929 Burton E. Stevenson's *Home Book of Verse for Young Folks* (1915, revised 1929), which by that time had become a standard reference collection of poetry, appeared in its present form. Two useful anthologies of poems carefully chosen for little children came out during the thirties—Mildred P. Harrington's *Ring-A-Round* (1930) and *Sung under the Silver Umbrella* (1935), a collection of poems selected by the Literature Committee of the Association for Childhood Education International. Both are well chosen and organized according to the interests of little children. The poems are uncrowded on the page, and the illustrations are imaginative and delicate. As the school began to recognize more clearly the relationship of poetry to the daily experiences of children, *My Poetry Book* (1934) by Grace T. Huffard and Laura M. Carlisle (with the collaboration of Helen Ferris) came as a welcome addition to compilations so organized as to facilitate such association. The same sprightliness, originality of design, and freshness in selection which characterized Louis Untermeyer's *This Singing World* (1923) appeared again in *Rainbow in the Sky* in 1935, prepared for children from six to twelve years of age. The introduction, which compares poetry to the rainbow, a sign of promise with a pot of gold at the end of it, is very usable with children. John E. Brewton's ever popular *Under the Tent of the Sky* (1937) saw the world of animals with the unfeigned delight of the children themselves.

The collections of verse available during the Golden Age of Children's Books came like a blaze of light into what had until 1915 been a darkened room. Moralizing was gone, and poetry was for delight.

THE LONG VIEW AND THE BROAD VIEW IN HISTORY AND GEOGRAPHY

History, too, flourished during these years. Virgil M. Hillyer, who in *A Child's History of the World* (1924) had helped to place the United States in its world setting for children, now contributed a second volume called *A Child's Geography of the World* (1929), in which he avoided, as he said, coming back from a country "with nothing

but a parrot and a string of beads."[127] His aim, as in the earlier volume, was to broaden the child's horizon and to help him to see his own country in relation to the rest of the world. Four years later he produced with Edward G. Huey *A Child's History of Art* (1933).[128] Its aim was to interest children in the masterpieces of painting, sculpture, and architecture. All three volumes are written with lively humor. They were revised with the aid of Mr. Huey in 1951.

Gertrude Hartman shared Mr. Hillyer's idea about the sweep of history as children should see it. To her, national history belonged after pupils were familiar with the world scene. And that they might understand the world scene, tracing it from its geological foundations to the present, understanding prehistoric times and following the course of peoples, of trade, of social organization, of aspirations and goals, she wrote three books invaluable for children: *The World We Live In and How It Came to Be* (1931), *These United States and How They Came to Be* (1932), and *Medieval Days and Ways* (1937). Profusely illustrated with maps and pictures, the books are for younger children than Van Loon's and Hillyer's histories are.

HISTORICAL FICTION FOR OLDER CHILDREN

Historical fiction was well represented during these years. Constance Lindsay Skinner was opening up the West to young readers in such stories as *Becky Landers, Frontier Warrior* (1926). James Boyd's *Drums* (1925), a tale of the American Revolution, and Charles B. Nordhoff and James N. Hall's *Falcons of France* (1929), an exciting story of World War I, were challenging more mature readers. Anne Carroll Moore at this time brought out her attractive edition of Washington Irving's *Knickerbocker's History of New York* (1928) with vigorous illustrations by James Daugherty—vigorous, that is, except when he was picturing Van Twiller! Eric P. Kelly's *The Trumpeter of Krakow* (1928) opened up little known aspects of Polish history in a story of great sympathy and idealism, for which he was awarded the Newbery Medal.

A NEW DISTINCTION IN BIOGRAPHY

The children's book world was enriched during this period by a number of notable biographies, distinguished by the same careful scholarship and felicity of style that characterize the best biographical writing for adults. Carl Sandburg's *Abe Lincoln Grows Up* (1928), with its uniquely interpretive illustrations by James Daugherty, brought to American boys and girls the story of Lincoln's youth from the early chapters of *Abraham Lincoln, the Prairie Years* (1926, two volumes; 1929, one volume). Its tone is contemplative, filled with the loneliness and the strength of the pioneer wilderness and the impact of both upon the spirit of a thoughtful youth.

Sandburg's biography was followed in 1933 by Cornelia Meigs's *Invincible Louisa*, the challenging story of a generous and impetuous girl, whose devotion to her family and lively sense of humor triumphed in spite of the privations and anxieties of her immediate environment. Would-be writers among the admirers of Louisa May Alcott never fail to find courage in her devotion to her task. Incidentally, they learn much from this penetrating biography of the times and literary world in which she lived.

In 1935 Elizabeth Janet Gray produced her *Young Walter Scott* (1935), a human and childlike story of the young Walter's overcoming his physical handicap and his growth to young manhood. It is told with unique appreciation of his boyish spirit and determination and of the Scottish background which played so important a part in his development.

The following year Constance Rourke presented a very different struggle for recognition in the life of Audubon (*Audubon,* 1936). His journeys in search of birds throughout Kentucky and Louisiana and his increasing skill in painting them were intimately associated with the understanding and encouragement of his wife.

In 1938 Jeanette Eaton made her debut as a writer of biography for young people in her much needed and scholarly biography of George Washington, *Leader by Destiny* (1938). Its emphasis is upon the gradual personal development of George Washington against the background of the Revolution in response to the demands of the situation in which he found himself.

The decade ended with James Daugherty's inimitable *Daniel Boone* (1939) told with

From *Daniel Boone* by James Daugherty.
Il. by author. Viking, 1939.

enthusiasm and great gusto in both story
and pictures. The two elements are so unified
in theme and in spirit as to be inseparable
one from the other. Daugherty's introductory
letter to Daniel Boone and his vigorous
address to the "lanky sons of democracy"
help to give youthful readers a sense of kin-
ship with the redoubtable hero of the
wilderness.[129]

All of these biographies present a challenge to good readers and to other writers
of more superficial biography which flourished during this period.

SCIENCE FOR YOUNG READERS

In the field of science, too, there has been
a steady increase in objectivity and scholarship in books for young people. As in the
field of history, recognized scientists from
this time on have not felt it beneath their
dignity to write for children. William Maxfield Reed, formerly professor of astronomy
at Harvard, wrote several valuable books
for his nine-year-old nephew, among them,
The Earth for Sam (1930) and *The Sea for
Sam* (1935), both of which were revised in
1960. *The Earth for Sam* describes successive geologic periods from the formation
of the earth to the caveman with descriptions
also of animal life. Wilfred S. Bronson, whose
Pollwiggle's Progress (1932), describing
stages in the life of a frog, had been full of
interest for children, cooperated in writing
The Sea for Sam, which deals with ocean-
ography, undersea life, and recent oceanic
discoveries. Bronson was a clever illustrator,
a staff artist of the Peabody Museum at Yale.
All these books contain unusually effective
photographs and drawings.

Raymond Ditmars of the American Museum of Natural History and the Bronx
Zoological Museum in 1933 did a new edition
of his *Reptiles of the World,* first published
in 1910. One of the most popular of books
about the stars was done by Professor Robert H. Baker of the University of Illinois
in 1934. It is called *When the Stars Come
Out.* Recent discoveries and telescopic im-
provements appear in the revision of 1954.
Robert and Jane Hegner's *Parade of the Ani-*

mal Kingdom (1935) is still a most useful book on the subject. In 1939 Harriet Huntington began her simple and suggestive series of picture books for primary grade children with *Let's Go Outdoors*, which invites them to discover how much can be learned observing little creatures in field and stream.

FURTHER EVIDENCE OF ACTIVITY IN THE FIELD OF CHILDREN'S BOOKS

During this period various organizations were at work stimulating a fuller use of books at home and in school. The Child Study Association of America had already begun its publication of helps for book selection under the direction of its Children's Book Committee, publishing in its *Child Study* magazine (1921-) lists of best books of the year for children.

By 1929 the Junior Literary Guild had been established under the direction of Helen Ferris and a distinguished advisory committee. In 1939, it produced a notable report of ten years of effort "to enrich young life" with good books sent monthly to children around the country—books chosen because of their special appeal to young readers.[130] Today, the organization serves five groups monthly from ages 5-6 through 12-16, with separate selections for boys and for girls in this upper range.

In 1936 a Library Service Division was created in the United States Office of Education under the efficient direction of Nora E. Beust. The purpose of the new division was to interpret the school library and its services to teachers and administrators, to the lay public, and to other supervisors and directors of the United States Office of Education. The practical nature of its contributions was soon demonstrated by the publication of a bulletin called *500 Books for Children* (1940), selected by Miss Beust.[131] The list aimed to help parents, classroom teachers, and librarians in homes and schools with limited funds to choose wisely the books most important for first purchase.

The Association for Childhood Education International early showed its interest in children's books and reading by publishing *A Bibliography of Books for Young Children* in 1937.[132] The list is still being published in biennial revisions. Successive issues of the ACEI bulletin of inexpensive books for children also appear from time to time. Articles on children's books and the stimulation of personal reading have appeared on occasion in *Childhood Education*, the monthly magazine of the association, since its inception.[133] The series of *Umbrella* books began in 1930 with *Told under the Green Umbrella* (old stories for new children) while the association was still known as the International Kindergarten Union. The literature committee appointed at that time sponsored several similar volumes like *Told under the Blue Umbrella* (new stories for new children, 1933), *Sung under the Silver Umbrella* (poetry, 1935), and *Told under Spacious Skies* (1952). The series resulted from the need for simple tellings of old and new tales for young children and for poetry adapted to the interests of little folks.

In 1937 the National Council of Teachers of English brought out its first reading list for elementary school children, *Reading for Fun,* which appeared under the chairmanship of Eloise Ramsey, then of Wayne University.[134] Successive revisions have now eventuated in a 1960 edition called *Adventuring with Books,* subject to revision every few years.[135] The 1960 edition was produced under the direction of Muriel Crosby, Assistant Superintendent of Schools in Wilmington, Delaware. Increased cooperation between schools and libraries was exemplified in a joint report of the National Education Association and the American Library Association called *Schools and Public Libraries Working Together in School Library Service.*[136] Meanwhile, Phyllis Fenner was exemplifying in her elementary school library in Manhasset, New York, how a school library could best be organized to maintain an inviting atmosphere as it served both the personal and the educational needs of boys and girls.[137]

Children's Books in World War II and Beyond—1940-1950

THE PLACE OF BOOKS IN THE WAR YEARS

The realm of children's books in the 1940's was beclouded by war. The book world took on the responsibility of maintaining old values and establishing new ones. Frederic G. Melcher's editorials in the annual children's book issue of *Publishers' Weekly* give a clear picture of the direction publishing took at this time. Books were to focus on the new areas of conflict—to inform children about our enemies and to introduce our friendly neighbors in Latin America.[138] A special effort was to be made to prevent other methods of communication from supplanting books.[139] We were to keep "reading as usual."[140] The story current in the book world was of the little cockney boy in an air raid shelter in London, lost in a book while bombs burst overhead. His irate mother snatched the book out of his hand. "Give over, Dannie," she demanded, "and pay h'attention to the war!"[141] Books were a "merry boon in a darkened world," said Mrs. De Lima. Books were to keep our established values before us—the good old books as well as the new ones that spoke of the dignity of the individual, regard for the human spirit, the necessity for individual freedom.[142] And this they did under very difficult circumstances.

It was at this time, also, that the Child Study Association of America established its "annual award for a book for children which deals realistically with problems in their contemporary world." "This award," writes Josette Frank, Director of Children's Books and Mass Media for the association, "was inaugurated during World War II when children were living through many difficult situations." Instructions to the committee were that "the book must present an honest treatment of its theme. It must be convincing and realistic in its approach and not too obviously purposeful. It should be a book which children will enjoy reading as a story, but in which they will also realize the deeper implications." Among the books which received this award during the 1940's was *The Big Wave* (1948) by Pearl Buck. In the 1950's Taro Yashima's *Crow Boy* (1955) and Virginia Sorensen's *Plain Girl* (1955) won awards.

In addition, since 1947, the Child Study Association of America has produced its series of anthologies of stories and verse for children, known as the *Read-to-Me* series, published by Thomas Y. Crowell.[143] These are valuable stories for use with young children in home, nursery school, and kindergarten.

Books sold, too, astonishingly well; just how well Miss Lesser of Doubleday reported after a trip around the book stores of the nation.[144] The quantity and quality were amazing, and there was money to pay for them. Numerous industrial workers who never before had had money to buy books now spent it gladly on their children's reading. The shortage of material for toys may also have increased the desirability of books. Book Week slogans of the war years were significant: 1943 *Build the Future with Books;* 1944 *United through Books;* 1945 *United through Books;* 1946 *Books Are Bridges.* As soon as peace was declared, books were to establish mutual understanding among the peoples of the world. And within one year an International Youth Book Exhibit was held in Munich beginning July 3, 1946, sponsored by the Information Control Division of the Office of the German Military Government. Fifteen nations cooperated, most of which were at war with Germany only a little more than a year before. "They were now willing," said the representative of the Information Service, "to contribute samples of their culture and traditions to help the youth of Germany rebuild towards a peaceful world."[145]

AMERICA AND AMERICANS IN CHILDREN'S BOOKS

It may be interesting to look first at the books about America and Americans. Mrs. Wilder continued her series on the pioneer days with *The Long Winter* (1940), *Little Town on the Prairie* (1941), and *These*

Happy Golden Years (1943). Walter D. Edmonds gave intermediate grade children one of their most dramatic stories of colonial fights with the Indians, with a child their own age as the hero. *The Matchlock Gun* (1941) won the Newbery Medal in 1942. The two most significant books setting forth the American dream for older boys and girls were Esther Forbes's *Johnny Tremain* (1943) and Rebecca Caudill's *Tree of Freedom* (1949). The first, the story of the growth in character and maturity of a boy as he played his part in the Revolutionary War, ends in Tom Paine's address to American youth of the future. The other presented a family moving westward carrying with them their tree of freedom, grown from a seed from Huguenot France. In the end, when a hostile arrow splintered its stalk, Stephanie took heart from the thought that it had good roots and would sprout again. "You couldn't kill freedom," she assured herself, "if somebody gave it uncommon good care."[146] Mr. Melcher wrote in 1943: "One thing is certain: The future we want must have its roots in the past and in the present."[147] Certainly these two books substantiate his thesis.

Understanding among the people who make up America was of paramount importance in these days. Many books of the 1940's pictured children who represented diversified backgrounds within the nation. Doris Gates's little heroine, the child of an itinerant worker, came to life for American children in *Blue Willow* (1940). In *Thee,*

Hannah! (1940) Marguerite de Angeli presented a lovable little Quaker girl of pre-Civil War days. Ann Nolan Clark also produced, with the help of the Tewa Indian children in the Southwest, the rhythmic story of life in an Indian community in *In My Mother's House* (1941) with exquisitely

From *In My Mother's House* by Ann Nolan Clark. Il. by Velino Herrera. Viking, 1941.

interpretive pictures by Velino Herrera. This she followed two years later with *Little Navajo Bluebird* (1943), an interpretation of Navajo Indian life today in the warm family story of a six-year-old child in a hogan. Eleanor Estes's *The Hundred Dresses* (1944) made real the problem of a little Polish girl in a so-called American community. Lois Lenski's *Strawberry Girl* (1945) among the Florida "crackers" is kin to any other child in America though the conditions of her life are very different.

Leo Politi appeared at this time with his deeply touching stories of the little Mexican children of Olvera Street in Los Angeles: *Pedro, the Angel of Olvera Street* (1946), who played the part of the angel in the Christmas pageant, and *Juanita* (1948) and the blessing of animals at Easter. Both gave evidence of the rich heritage our children enjoy from their forebears of other lands. But most important, each of these children was a real personality in his own right.

American folk songs appeared in two distinguished volumes—Carl Carmer's *America Sings* (1942) and Ruth Crawford Seeger's *American Folk Songs for Children* (1948), both attractively illustrated. Perhaps the greatest contribution of all was Richard Chase's recording for American boys and girls of the authentic folklore of the southern mountains in *Jack Tales* (1943) and *Grandfather Tales* (1948). It is amazing, as one looks back, how in spite of the war, "reading as usual" was not forgotten. Robert McCloskey came forth with two "real boys" who gave both boys and girls a good laugh. *Lentil* (1940), however, is much more than a funny book. Its picture of the return of "the politician" from Washington and how Lentil saved the day with his harmonica is as authentic Americana as it is good humor. *Homer Price* (1943), who jumped from one predicament into another always to come out on top, is as real a boy as our country has produced. He needs no advertis-

ing—mere mention of his name produces a grin. Incidentally, the scene is unmistakably American.

Then he let out a loud chuckle and began to sing "Driving Six White Horses When She Comes."

From *Lentil* by Robert McCloskey. Il. by author. Viking, 1940.

At the opening of the decade came two family stories as true-to-life and as American as could be found in the annals of children's books in any generation. One was Eleanor Estes's *The Moffats* (1941), a story filled with humor and warm family feeling. The other was Elizabeth Enright's *The Saturdays* (1941), the entertaining story of four children in New York City who pooled their allowances each Saturday so that once a month each of them spent all the family wealth, that is, the children's share of it. The spread in age permits an interesting view of the heart's desires of each of them.

CHILDREN AROUND THE WORLD

Stories of children around the world continued to appear in books as distinguished in format as in content. The hilarious adventure of a little Chinese boy who received a kite in the shape of a fish for his birthday delights the heart of every would-be fisherman in the kindergarten and primary grades (Kurt Wiese, *Fish in the Air,* 1948). Two stories for older readers were of fearful boys who proved their courage as they came of age—Mafatu, the Polynesian boy in Armstrong Sperry's *Call It Courage* (1940), and the hero of *Li Lun, Lad of Courage* (1947) in Carolyn Treffinger's story of China. The first was replete with adventure on the Pacific in a small catamaran, a meeting with head hunters, and many other hair-raising events. The second revealed the courage and loneliness of a boy without companions on a mountain peak, challenging sun and shrieking birds as he guarded his kernels of rice. Tibet is the scene of Louise Rankin's *Daughter of the Mountains* (1948), the story of the little girl who followed a caravan all the way to Calcutta to rescue her golden haired dog, which had been stolen. Ruth Sawyer showed similar knowledge of Mexico in her revelation of the comradeship between a little Mexican boy and his donkey in *The Least One* (1941). The tempo of the book is slow, even as life in Mexico is slow; in this and other respects the author revealed a unique knowledge of her subject. Claire Huchet Bishop, in her *Pancakes—Paris* (1947) offered a story filled with laughter and tears as it related the encounters of American soldiers with a destitute French family that had suffered greatly in the war. Finally, Pearl Buck's *The Big Wave* (1948) revealed simply and poignantly the sorrow of a Japanese boy whose family was lost in a tidal wave and his struggle to overcome his grief.

RECREATING OLDEN TIMES

Three books of historical fiction written during this decade deserve special mention: Elizabeth Janet Gray's *Adam of the Road* (1942), Eleanore M. Jewett's *The Hidden Treasure of Glaston* (1946), and Marguerite de Angeli's *The Door in the Wall* (1949). All three presented sound historical background of the Middle Ages and captured the spirit of the times. The stories moved slowly because life itself moved slowly in those days. *The Hidden Treasure of Glaston,* against a background of medieval times in the famous abbey of Glastonbury, told the adventures of two boys in search of hidden treasures connected with King Arthur and his quest for the Holy Grail. *Adam of the Road* was filled with minstrelsy, great cathedrals, life on the road and in the castles at which Adam's father sang and played. Adam meanwhile lent excitement to the story by his pursuit of his lost dog, after which he was reunited with his father. *The Door in the Wall* is a very different story of how the crippled son of a lord triumphed over his handicap and won his spurs—not in battle but through an act of great courage.

NEW ASPECTS OF HISTORY AND GEOGRAPHY

In the previous decade, just as Hendrik W. Van Loon, Virgil M. Hillyer, and Gertrude Hartman had reinterpreted the past and its relation to the present, so Genevieve Foster introduced a horizontal approach to history in her *George Washington's World* (1941), *Abraham Lincoln's World* (1944), and *Augustus Caesar's World* (1947). In these books, children who already knew something of the America of George Washington and Abraham Lincoln saw their country's history in the light of contemporaneous events elsewhere in the world. In *Augustus Caesar's World,* in which the beginning of Christianity played a part, children found a solid footing in geography and history for the places and events of the New Testament.

Holling C. Holling's *Paddle-to-the-Sea* (1941) dramatized in the experiences of the little carved Indian in his canoe, the journey from Nipigon to Europe, now made a reality in the opening of the St. Lawrence Seaway; whereas his *Tree in the Trail* (1942) led boys and girls back to the story of the Santa Fe Trail. Two other books of history were of special interest at this time: Anne Terry White's *Lost Worlds* (1941), the story of archeology and its unearthing of buried civilizations, and Helen Follett's *Ocean Outposts* (1942), which had special relevance at the moment because it dealt with the Philippines, Guam, and other Pacific Islands.

Two easier books followed which were especially useful for intermediate grade his-

tory and geography: Roger Duvoisin's graphically illustrated *They Put Out to Sea* (1944), a simple narrative of traders, explorers, and conquerors from the Phoenicians

From *They Put Out to Sea* by Roger Duvoisin. Il. by author. Knopf, 1944.

to Magellan; and May McNeer's *The Story of the Southwest* (1948), presenting in attractive, almost picture book format, the backgrounds, people, and customs of the southwestern part of our country.

A NEW VARIETY IN BIOGRAPHY

Perhaps the most significant advance in children's books of these years was in biography. Every war tends to be accompanied and followed by an array of books designed to arouse patriotic sentiments or at least to help children understand the ideals which our country seeks to defend. In this case, books of real stature began to appear about our own heroes. Jeanette Eaton presented with a rich array of facts and great skill in the delineation of character the lives of *Narcissa Whitman, Pioneer of Oregon* (1941), of Roger Williams in *Lone Journey* (1944), and of *That Lively Man, Ben Franklin* (1948).

Robert Lawson, in 1940, produced with his vigorous line and sprightly humor *They Were Strong and Good,* the story of the ancestors of one American boy on both his father's and his mother's side of the family. James Daugherty still maintained his boyhood enthusiasm for Americana in *Poor Richard* (1941) and *Abraham Lincoln* (1943). Esther Averill did her delightful *Daniel Boone* (1945) with its intimate little pictures of the Kentucky pioneer days in marginal drawings by Rojankovsky. Esther Forbes added to the pictorial series of American heroes with lavish illustration and abbreviated text *America's Paul Revere* (1946), which was followed by Stewart Holbrook's

America's Ethan Allen (1949). Both were distinguished for their dramatic pictures by Lynd Ward. These short biographies, it was hoped, could be translated readily for use in presenting the heroes of democracy to the children of other nations.

Alongside these accounts of great Americans, Anna G. Hall's impressive revelation of the genius, the courage, and the accomplishments of the explorer, Fridtjof Nansen (*Nansen,* 1940), stands out as one of the great biographies of the decade. The wide spread both in subject and in difficulty represented in the biographies of this period is well exemplified in the stories of artists, musicians, and showmen which appeared for younger readers in Opal Wheeler's *Stephen Foster and His Little Dog Tray* (1941) and *Ludwig Beethoven and the Chiming Tower Bells* (1942), in Mabel Leigh Hunt's *Have You Seen Tom Thumb?* (1942), the story of the famous midget in P. T. Barnum's circus, and in Marguerite Henry's *Benjamin West and His Cat, Grimalkin* (1947).

Other needed informative materials for middle grade children appeared at this time. The field of music, in addition to being represented in biography, was enriched by the appearance of Harriet Huntington's *Tune-Up; The Instruments of the Orchestra and Their Players* (1942), which has remained a standard work for twenty years. Children's appreciation of their own religions and those of other peoples was greatly enhanced by the three significant contributions of Florence Fitch: *One God; The Ways We Worship Him* (1944), an objective presentation of Catholic, Protestant, and Jewish faiths; *Their Search for God; Ways of Worship in the Orient* (1947); and *Allah, the God of Islam* (1950). In 1950, also, Delight Ansley made a similar contribution to older children in her single volume, *The Good Ways* (1950).

From *McElligot's Pool* by Dr. Suess. Il. by author. Random, 1947.

THE PICTURE BOOK IN THE FORTIES

In spite of the fact that many artists and writers were involved in World War II, the output of picture books during the decade (1940-49) as a whole was remarkable for its variety of form and theme. In 1941 Hans A. Rey's *Curious George,* the boisterous monkey whose lively antics have proved a good substitute for the comics, appeared on the scene to brighten the war years for little children. Dr. Seuss produced *Horton Hatches the Egg* (1940) and later *McElligot's Pool* (1947), in which a small boy's aspirations as a fisherman matched those of his readers. The gay colors and lively,

From *Curious George* by H. A. Rey. Il. by author. Houghton, 1941.

original designs still delight the hearts of young fishermen.

Robert McCloskey's *Make Way for Ducklings* (1941) has given a new distinction to the Hub of the Universe. Families from all

From *Make Way for Ducklings* by Robert McCloskey. Il. by author. Viking, 1941.

over the country visit Boston annually to spot the place where the ducklings had their nest. The author's insight into the care of the mother duck for her brood, the meticulous attention he gave to drawing each individual duck as it appears from picture to picture, the background of Boston Gardens as seen through the eyes of a duck, and above all, the duck's-eye view of the Irish policeman, who dominates the scene—all show the humor, the knowledge of children, and the care for infinite detail which place this story among the indispensable classics of childhood. The glee of the children knows no bounds when the proud mother and her none-too-steady little ones walk calmly across Charles Street, while all the traffic of

Boston waits. *Blueberries for Sal* (1948) with its exchange of mothers by Sal and the baby bear is particularly popular with children of the north woods, who know the incident could have happened.

Virginia Lee Burton's *The Little House*

From *The Little House* by Virginia Lee Burton. Il. by author. Houghton, 1942.

(1942) is also a great picture book personalizing in terms of another "small one" a fundamental fact of sociology. The imaginative presentation of the happy little house in the apple orchard on the hilltop and its sad transformation under the elevated railroad as the great city moves out and surrounds it make this one of the most original of American picture books. The delicacy of color and the graceful design fit the theme perfectly. In the same year came Mary and Conrad

Buff's rhythmically told story of two little fawns, Dash and Dart (*Dash and Dart*, 1942) who grow through the year. The exquisite double-page spreads in the greens and browns of the forest give way to a beautiful white snow as the seasons progress. The picture book is a must for kindergarten and primary grade children. Virginia Burton's *Katy and the Big Snow* (1943) added another to the procession of animated machines begun in the thirties. Another star in the picture book firmament appeared in 1944—Marie Ets with her *In the Forest*. The gay childlike quality of the story and the humorous masterly drawings of the animals make every detail a joy to the children.

Two very different picture books with a winter theme won the Caldecott Award toward the end of the decade. Alvin Tresselt's graphic *White Snow, Bright Snow* (1947), with pictures by Roger Duvoisin, showed the beauty of the snow-covered landscape coupled with responsibilities resulting from the storm for the postman, the policeman, and other people of the community. Berta and Elmer Hader, on the other hand, in *The Big Snow* (1948) pictured what the first snowfall of the season meant to the animals of the forest.

IMAGINATIVE STORIES FOR THE MIDDLE GRADES

Imaginative stories for the middle grades were equally rich in output. The effort of some publishers to keep up the quality of children's books in wartime is evident from the fact that these stories are distributed rather evenly throughout the decade. Arna Bontemps and Jack Conroy brought out their hilarious tale of *The Fast Sooner Hound* (1942) who "got there" ahead of the railroad train. James Thurber's *Many Moons* (1943), the fanciful story of how the court jester secured the moon for the little princess, has just the right pictures in Louis Slobodkin's dreamlike interiors. Robert Lawson's *Rabbit Hill* (1944) is already a classic, revealing the life of the rabbits and the tiny creatures in the garden of the big house.

From *Rabbit Hill* by Robert Lawson. Il. by author. Viking, 1944.

The dignity and grace with which he presents the little animals are combined with just enough good-natured satire to make both story and pictures a delight. Strictly for girls is Carolyn G. Bailey's *Miss Hickory* (1946), the New Hampshire doll with a hickory nut head and an apple twig body. New England in character and in love of the out-of-doors, she emerges a real personality.

In a class all by itself is William Pène DuBois's *Twenty-One Balloons* (1947), the story of Professor Sherman's journey by balloon to the island home of the most original of inventors, who have contrived even to invent an instrument of escape from the inevitable volcanic eruption which befalls their island. The drawings are compounded of mathematics and magic.

A welcome relief from the solemnity of many books of the day was *My Father's Dragon* by Ruth Stiles Gannett (1948). It is an hilarious extravaganza in which a small boy proudly relates his father's cleverness in dealing with the animals of a jungle island who hold captive a pathetic little dragon and force him to act as an airlift to the mainland. The grand climax comes when the crocodile bridge drops into the sea as the animals are on their way across in pursuit of "Father," thus ending the story with speed and finality. The next year saw the appearance of a very different book, Rutherford Montgomery's delightful *Kildee House* (1949). For the sake of seclusion, Mr. Kildee had built his house against a giant redwood tree, but he was not alone long. Grouch, the raccoon, and a family of skunks moved in. The problem of overpopulation soon became acute. Efforts to solve it were compounded of humor and a clear sense of the individuality of the animals.

MYTHS, HERO STORIES, AND FAIRY TALES

In the midst of all these modern materials, the hero stories, the myths, and the legends were not forgotten. Babette Deutsch did her poetic retelling of the *Heroes of the Kalevala* (1940); Helen Sewell did illustrations for *A Book of Myths; Selections from Bulfinch's Age of Fable* (1942); Dorothy Hosford produced her vigorous *Beowulf*, called *By His Own Might* (1947); and Virginia Lee Burton illustrated Anne Malcolmson's *Song of Robin Hood* (1947), with musical accompaniment by Grace Castagnetta. *Yankee Doodle's Cousins* (1941), a collection of tales of the "obstreperous heroes of America," collected by Anne Malcolmson and illustrated by Robert McCloskey, remains a favorite with boys and girls. Harold Felton's *Pecos Bill, Texas Cow Puncher* (1949) and a new edition of Glen Rounds's *Ol' Paul, the Mighty Logger* (1949) added valuable material about these two popular heroes.

At this time, also, Virginia Lee Burton did her exquisite little book of Hans Christian Andersen's *The Emperor's New Clothes* (1949) and Wanda Ga'g produced her *Three Gay Tales from Grimm* (1943). Of the "tongues" speaking to our children of the story lore of other lands the most notable were Roger Duvoisin's in *The Three Sneezes and Other Swiss Tales* (1941), Alice Kelsey's in the Turkish stories in *Once the Hodja* (1943), and Sigrid Undset's in *True and Untrue and Other Norse Tales* (1945).

MORE POETRY IN THE FORTIES

John E. Brewton, during this decade, added to his popular and carefully selected anthologies of verse *Gaily We Parade* (1940), poems of people, and *Bridled with Rainbows* (1949), verses about "many things of earth and sky," the latter in collaboration with his wife, Sara Brewton. Both volumes serve a very real purpose in the classroom throughout the elementary school program. Louis Untermeyer, also, added to his collections already described an equally attractive volume, *Stars to Steer By* (1941) for grades 6 through 9.

Maud and Miska Petersham presented to American children in 1945 *The Rooster Crows,* a collection of rhymes, games, and jingles which had delighted boys and girls in this country for generations. The interest in them was greatly enhanced by the delightfully humorous pictures. Barbara P. Geismer and Antoinette B. Suter's *Very Young Verses* (1945) and Gladys Adshead's *An Inheritance of Poetry* (1948) fulfilled two very different functions: the first being a collection of simple verses about the everyday interests of nursery school children, and the second introducing distinguished poems of American and English literature for use by teachers in reading aloud and for more gifted readers to read for themselves.

A NEW ARRAY OF ANIMAL STORIES

An extraordinary array of good animal stories came out during the forties. The first two were much more than dog stories.

Lassie Come-Home (1940) by Eric Knight centered not only in the collie dog but also in the close family ties of father and son. It was further enriched by the descriptions of the Scottish highlands and the English countryside through which Lassie made her way back to Yorkshire after having been sold to a Scotch landlord.

Mutual understanding between father and son also characterized *My Friend Flicka* (1941) by Mary Sture-Vasa (pseud. Mary O'Hara), the sensitively told story of a boy and his pet colt. Against the background of a Wyoming ranch, Ken proved that his choice of colt was right.

Marguerite Henry's love of a thoroughbred and a well-won race is at the heart of all her horse stories. Her great care in the use of details and her deep sense of the part played by place and time in her stories make reading her *King of the Wind* (1948) and *Misty of Chincoteague* (1947) an unforgettable experience for boys and girls.

From *King of the Wind* by Marguerite Henry. Il. by Wesley Dennis. Rand, 1948.

The story of Godolphin Arabian, ancestor of Man o' War, and his journey with his deaf-mute stable boy is a poignant one, coming to a grand climax in the finding of a mate in England. *Misty*, too, the story of a horse descended from the Moorish ponies that escaped from a Spanish galleon, is spectacularly set in the waters around Chincoteague. These books ushered in a new day in horse stories.

In Glen Rounds's *The Blind Colt* (1941), Whitey's faith in his blind colt is justified when the animal learns to be his "Sunday horse." Jim Kjelgaard in *Big Red* (1945) meets the challenge of less gifted readers who cannot appreciate the flavor of Marguerite Henry's prose. They can, however, follow excitedly this simpler tale of the Irish setter who ultimately overcame the bear among the sheep of the western mountains. The deftness of the boy's handling of the setter adds greatly to the suspense of the story.

SCIENCE AND INVENTION IN CHILDREN'S BOOKS

By the end of World War II interest was high in science and invention. Even little children had science books of their own with concepts developed in text and in illustration suited to the level of their understanding. Irma E. Webber's *Up Above and Down Below* (1943) is an ingenious presentation for preschool children of plants and animals which live above and beneath the earth's surface. Her *Travelers All* (1944)

gives a distinctly imaginative touch to the story of how plants travel, and her *Bits That Grow Big* (1949) affords children a taste of real experimentation. Alvin Tresselt's *Rain Drop Splash* (1946), with colorful pictures by Leonard Weisgard, shows why it would be tragic if rain never came to keep children indoors. Many other attractive picture books like Margaret Wise Brown's (pseud. Golden MacDonald) *The Little Island* (1946) contribute directly to the child's understanding of science. So also do other artistic nature books for older children like Mary and Conrad Buff's *The Big Tree* (1946) in which the long life of a sequoia tree is filled with wonder and beauty as animals and the centuries come and go.

Lois Lenski endeared herself to preschool children with her diminutive picture books about *The Little Airplane* (1938), *The Little Train* (1940), and *The Little Farm* (1942), all of them now published by Henry Z. Walck, Incorporated. Harriet E. Huntington's series continued to attract little children with *Let's Go to the Desert*, published in 1949. Addison Webb's *Birds in Their Homes* (1947) satisfies the curiosity of children about nests and the birds' care of their young. A useful and authentic series with excellent photographs was Henry B. Kane's *Wild World* tales (1940-49), among the most serviceable of which were *The Tale of the Whitefoot Mouse* (1940), *The Tale of the Bullfrog* (1941), *The Tale of the Promethea Moth* (1942), and *The Tale* of the Wild Goose (1946). These books served an important purpose as long as they were in print. The value of Harper and Row's *Basic Science Education* series (1941-   ) has been recognized throughout the schools. As the demand for supplementary materials in science for both primary and intermediate grades increases, these pamphlets continue to meet the needs of children for colorful and authentic helps for the study of the natural world.

The *First Book* series had begun to make itself felt in the area of science, one of the most useful titles being Margaret Williamson's *First Book of Bugs* (1949). Two standard works for older pupils also appeared at this time: *The Animal Book, American Mammals North of Mexico* by Dorothy C. Hogner (1942, revised by Walck 1958), and Hilda T. Harpster's *The Insect World* (1947). Other writers, also, like Jerome S. Meyer, Mae and Ira Freeman, and Herman and Nina Schneider were specializing in books of practical experiments for older pupils.

At this time, too, Herbert S. Zim, then a professor of biology at the University of Illinois, began his career as a writer for children. His *Elephants* (1946) and *Snakes* (1949) reveal his ability to tell boys and girls what they want to know in simple and authentic fashion with clear, accurate drawings. *Homing Pigeons* (1949) is an example of the practical handbooks Dr. Zim was to present on the housing, feeding, and breeding of animals. By 1949, too, John B. Lewel-

len was beginning his contribution to the field of atomic research. *You and Atomic Energy and Its Wonderful Uses* (1949) gave young readers a clear idea of what atomic energy is and how it can be used to benefit mankind.

The development of scientific research in many areas during and after World War II is reflected in the notable growth of interest in children's books in this area. In the following decade the expansion of the publishing program was to be even greater, in the areas of atomic research, of exploration by satellite, and of interplanetary investigations.

A VARIETY OF ACTIVITY BOOKS

During this decade many books of other kinds of activities appeared like Kurt Wiese's ingenious *You Can Write Chinese* (1945) and Herbert Zim's *Codes and Secret Writing* (1948). Opal Wheeler also added several interesting pictorial albums of music: *Sing for Christmas* (1943) and *Sing for America* (1944), both with illustrations by Gustav Tenggren, and *Sing Mother Goose* (1945) illustrated by Marjorie Torrey.

COOPERATION OF THE AMERICAN INSTITUTE OF GRAPHIC ARTS

Finally, it was during this decade which did so much to increase the breadth of subject matter in children's books that the American Institute of Graphic Arts began its distinctive service to the improvement of the general format and artistic design of the books themselves. In 1940, the Institute held its first Exhibition of Children's Books, chosen from the publications of 1937-40, at the newly opened Junior Museum of the Metropolitan Museum of Art. Ninety-nine books appeared from the many which had been judged for "excellence of design, printing, and general format with reference to the handling of subject matter and the limitations imposed by price."[148] The books were chosen by a jury composed of a children's librarian, a children's editor and designer, a representative of the printing arts, and a distinguished artist and illustrator. This was the first of a series of such exhibits, designed to bring before members of the children's book world qualities of excellence in the format of books. Each exhibit held has been accompanied by an illustrated brochure which sets forth the reasons for the choice of each title and presents a general overall picture of the merits and defects of books brought out during the years specified.[149] At the close of each exhibit in New York, the collection is sent throughout the country, wherever libraries or art galleries wish to display it. There is no doubt but that this periodic display has done much to alert publishers and purchasers of books to qualities of format and illustration which differentiate a distinguished book from a mediocre one.

Children's Books in a Bursting World—1950-1960

The decade from 1950 to 1960 was characterized by a strange conglomeration of trends, some of which are as difficult to define as to discern. More artists from Europe, like Fritz Eichenberg, Marc Simont, and Hans Fischer gave a new emphasis and distinctive art form to children's picture books after World War II. Achievements in science revealed a new universe, which aroused both wonder and the desire to know and to understand. Hitherto unheard-of nations appeared in the news, on motion picture, radio, and television, and in current books and periodicals. Early in the decade the *Saturday Review* published a cartoon presenting a boy engrossed in a television performance, a closer view of which he had achieved by sitting on top of a pile of encyclopedias. Teachers, publishers, and librarians banded together to show youthful readers the relationship between what was on the screen and what was in the encyclopedias.

THE IMMEDIACY OF THE URGE TO KNOW

Differences in reading ability among children. The immediacy of the urge to know created a demand for readable books of information on a wide variety of subjects. The word, "readable," had a dual significance. Information had to be presented for children of all ages in both authentic and interesting fashion if boys and girls were to be enticed to read it. On the other hand, research in reading had proved that children in the schools varied greatly in their ability to read, and that no amount of effort and no increase in scientifically devised materials would ever make identical reading material suitable for all of them. Hence came the need to provide scientific, geographical, and historical books on different levels of difficulty. There was a twofold challenge: first, to spur the gifted on to greater heights and depths in reading, and second, to provide less difficult but mature and authentic materials for boys and girls whose age and level of maturity exceeded their ability to read.

Another trend in the publishing of children's books had its inception in the newly aroused public concern for the teaching of beginning reading and for the expansion of individual reading beyond textbook materials. One fortunate outcome of this movement was the appearance of attractive, lively "easy" books, controlled in vocabulary, yet full of interest and well illustrated at their best, but sometimes silly and insulting to the intelligence of children and wooden in story and illustration at their worst.

The need for foreign languages. Then came the consciousness that Americans as a people were deficient in ability to use languages other than their own. A drive followed to prepare easy reading materials in French and Spanish, especially suitable for children now learning foreign languages in the elementary school. A tremendous impetus to the publication of books in science and languages came from the National Defense Education Act in which government funds were available to help schools acquire more books in these two areas of instruction.[150]

The challenge of the new "series." Still another movement was the production of books in series like the *Childhood of Famous Americans* (Bobbs, 1942- , earlier called *Boyhood of Famous Americans*) and the *First Book* series (Watts, 1944-), which were followed by *Landmark* books (Random, 1950-), *Real* books (Garden City Books, 1951-), *Signature* books (Grosset, 1952-), *True* books (Childrens Press, 1953-), *All-about* books (Random, 1953-), *Let's Visit* books (Day, 1956-), and *I-Want-to-Be* books (Childrens Press, 1956-), some of them good and some of them very sketchy, some well printed and securely bound, and some on poor paper and ready to fall apart. The general scheme of the *Landmark* books, one of the best and most popular series on the market, is told in "The Landmark Story," which appeared in *Publishers' Week-*

ly for July 30, 1956. The plan was to publish a series of books on "men, movements, and moments in history" associated with "turning points or landmarks in our national life."[151] Ten books a year were to be produced in a single format, at a uniform price, within a fixed time limit required by the production schedule, and at a prescribed level of difficulty. In this case, the level of difficulty was to be suited to the ability of good and superior readers in the upper years of the elementary schools. The facts were to be authentic and the stories dramatically told, so that from the point of view of interest and style, the books would not be beneath the concern of adults. The most distinguished authors available were to be found to deal with each subject. Dorothy Canfield Fisher wrote the first volume on *Paul Revere and the Minute Men* (1950) and James Daugherty, the story of *The Landing of the Pilgrims* (1950).

But ten volumes a year are difficult to maintain at a uniform standard of excellence. Important writers could do little else if they yielded to the present demands of the publishers. The relative significance of the subjects presented likewise varies after the production of an extended series of ten-volume sets. Yet children wait for "the next *Landmark* book" much as an older generation waited for "the next *Little Colonel* book" or "the next *Tom Swift* title."

Such was the success of the *Landmark* venture that the entire publishing world was fired by a desire to do likewise. *Publishers'*

Weekly for July, 1962, lists one hundred and thirty-five series now on the market.[152] Some of them have excellent scientific and historical titles in them like certain of the *First Book* series, for example. Others have special usefulness for beginning readers like Else H. Minarik's *Little Bear* (1957-) stories, Syd Hoff's *Danny and the Dinosaur* (1958), or Elizabeth Guilfoile's *Nobody Listens to Andrew* (1957), to name some of the best available. But advertising frequently talks in terms of "sets," and books are soon known by "brand" names such as *The James Brown Company's Easy Book Series.*[153] It is inevitable that in the tremendous multiplication of series, some are thin and pedestrian and others contain books of major significance. Some have a maximum of talk or action while others offer children both intensity and vitality of details.

The value of this entire publishing movement depends upon the intelligence of the teacher and librarian in resisting "brand" labels, in refusing "boxed sets," and in choosing wisely *each individual book on its own merits* after comparison with other available books on the same subject. For example, in the fall of 1960 twenty-four different editions of *Treasure Island* were on the market, some of them abridged, some unabridged, and many adapted for special groups of readers. The prices ranged from thirty-five cents to $3.95.[154] Two new biographies of Abraham Lincoln were added to the thirty-seven juveniles already available about him.

The whole situation presents a new challenge to purchasers of children's books to select each title on its merits for a particular reader or for a particular purpose. Individuality of format is also an important factor in the child's own choice of reading material. The problem is the more serious because better titles frequently have to be allowed to lapse in order to make room for the new and untried. In the field of "easy" books, several studies have been made to help the chooser.[155] The *Children's Catalog*, put out by the H. W. Wilson Company (1961), also distinguishes the better from the inferior titles. So do *The Horn Book Magazine* and *Elementary English* in their monthly reviews of books. The *Library Journal* and *School Library Journal* (formerly *Junior Libraries*) likewise review children's books monthly.[156] Especially helpful are the various publications of the American Library Association, such as its *A Basic Book Collection for Elementary Grades* and its *Notable Children's Books of the Year,* published by the Book Evaluation Committee of the Children's Services Division of the American Library Association, which appears annually in the April issue of the *American Library Association Bulletin.*[157] The elementary reading list, *Adventuring with Books,* is put out periodically with supplements by the National Council of Teachers of English.[158]

THE UNIVERSITY OF CHICAGO CENTER FOR CHILDREN'S BOOKS

In 1950 the Center for Children's Books was established by Frances Henne under the auspices of the Graduate Library School at the University of Chicago for the purpose of reviewing critically not only recommended books published each year, but inferior books as well, the weaknesses of which are clearly set forth for the purchaser. The latter service is particularly valuable for teachers and librarians who have difficulty seeing individual titles before ordering them. The fact that each book is discussed by a committee of experienced librarians gives support to the standards of evaluation. In addition, the editor has as resource persons the faculties of the University of Chicago and its laboratory school children and staff, so that there is opportunity to test such textual qualities as accuracy, comprehensiveness, and appropriateness by the opinions of experts and the reactions of children. The broad sweep of the collection makes it valuable for those who deal with less able and more matter-of-fact children as well as with the gifted and highly imaginative ones. In addition to an indication of grade placement, special symbols are used to designate *Recommended, Marginal,* and *Not Recommended* books, those useful as *Additional Acquisitions* for an already well-stocked school library, those chiefly valuable for *Specialized Collections,* and those appropriate mainly for the *Superior Reader.* Grade levels range from the preschool years through the junior high school. Mary K. Eakin was editor of the *Bulletin of the Center for Children's Books* until 1958. The present editor is Zena Bailey.[159]

THE OVERSIZED BOOKS

Another publishing trend which, although it had begun earlier, expanded in the 1950's was the appearance of the oversized book like the *Giant Golden* books (1951-) and the *Wonderful World* books (1955-). Important science titles appeared in this format, such as Bertha M. Parker's *The Golden Treasury of Natural History* (1952) and Donald Peattie's *The Rainbow Book of Nature* (1957). Lancelot Hogben's *The Wonderful World of Energy* (1957) and Benjamin Britten's *The Wonderful World of Music* (1958) also profited from the opportunity for extended treatment, profuse and colorful illustration, and the use of graphs, diagrams, and drawings possible in larger volumes.

MORE SERVICE FROM LIBRARIANS

During this period, too, librarians continued to work for the improvement of library service for children. Mildred L. Batchelder, throughout the 1950's, rendered efficient service as Executive Secretary of the Children's Services Division and the Young Adult Services Division of the American Library Association. Mary Peacock Douglas should also be remembered for her work and her writing on the development of school libraries, especially in the South.[160]

In 1960 the notable service of Frances Henne and Ruth Ersted to the raising of standards of school libraries climaxed in the preparation of a bulletin on standards for school library services. In it the library program for schools was described as giving "instruction, service, and activity throughout the school rather than merely within the four walls of the library quarters —a service rendered to teachers as well as to pupils, and including supplementary materials, equipment for listening and viewing, reference services, and guidance for personal reading."[161] The minimum annual book budget agreed upon, exclusive of reference books and a professional book collection for teachers, was $4.00 to $6.00 per pupil with slight variation for schools with enrollments of fewer than two hundred and fifty pupils.

THE RISE OF CHILDREN'S BOOK CLUBS

The 1950's saw the rise of numerous children's book clubs which have joined forces with school and home in making books available to young readers. In 1953 the *Weekly Reader Children's Book Club*[162] was organized, its lists including among their best titles Lynd Ward's *The Biggest Bear* and Ellen MacGregor's *Miss Pickerell Goes to Mars*. Today its program has expanded to include three levels of service: Kindergarten through Grade 2, Grades 3 and 4, and Grades 5 and 6. A year later the *Parents' Magazine's Book Club for Boys & Girls*[163] began its program with books for young readers from eight to twelve. Today, at the insistence of parents, it serves four levels of readers—the *Calling All Girls Book Club* and the *American Boys Book Club* for intermediate grade children, a *Book Club for Beginning Readers* and a *Read Aloud Book Club*. Beverly Cleary's *Henry and the Paper Route,* Thomas Handforth's *Mei Li,* Ruth S. Gannett's *My Father's Dragon,* and Sidonie M. Gruenberg's *Favorite Stories Old and New* are among its best offerings.

A *Catholic Children's Book Club,* which has been in operation since 1945, serves parochial schools of the country.[164] The work of the *Junior Literary Guild,* established by Helen Ferris in 1929, has already been referred to (p. 47). The Book-of-the-Month Club's juvenile division, *Young Readers of America Book Club,*[165] disseminates titles from the *Landmark* series and the *Allabout* books of Random House, which furnish largely informative books or fiction related to historical and scientific interests for children nine to thirteen.

THE COMING OF PAPERBACKS

The appearance of paperbacks for children is another aspect of the increased demand for books in the last decade. The *Arrow Book Club* of the Scholastic Book Services has helped greatly to stimulate personal reading in the schools and to make books available in the home.[166] Personal ownership of books often begins with paperbacks. Among the best titles in the program are *Homer Price, Grimm's Fairy Tales,* and *The Five Chinese Brothers,* in addition to many informative books like Zim's *The Great Whales* and *Codes and Secret Writing.* The

publishers also are becoming interested in the production of paperbacks for children, as, for example, Scribner's recent issue of Kenneth Grahame's *The Wind in the Willows* and Macmillan's *Call of the Wild* by Jack London. Rights for reproduction of good paperbacks may become increasingly difficult to secure as the publishers themselves enter the field. Hence, special care needs to be taken to select the best wherever they may be found. Paperbacks will never take the place of the original, beautiful editions such as are described in this monograph. They may be used, however, to whet the appetite for more reading of good books and to supply books in homes where they would not otherwise be available. Rightly used in home and in school, they may arouse pride in personal ownership of books, they may greatly increase the amount of wholesome reading done by boys and girls, and they may be stepping stones to the ownership and reading of many books which represent the heights in illustration and bookmaking already discussed here. They will stimulate among children the exchange and discussion of infinitely better books than the comic stands have been furnishing for a long time.

MORE GOOD PICTURE BOOKS

In spite of all these additions to the children's book supply, picture books continued to flourish in the 1950's. "The good picture story book," say the writers of *A Critical History of Children's Literature,* "has extraordinary powers of joy and enrichment, for the good ones add the beauty, humor, and appropriateness of their artistic interpretation to stories told with skill, imagination, and appreciation of fine words."[167] The decade from 1950 to 1960 was blessed with many picture books which lived up to these standards. Their originality and variety in both theme and technique were impressive. Some of them dealt with the everyday experiences of children like Katherine Milhous's *The Egg Tree* (1950), which revealed in graphic pictures and colorful folk designs the Easter celebration of the Pennsylvania Dutch, and Janice M. Udry's *A Tree Is Nice* (1956), depicting not only the beauty and usefulness of trees but the supreme joy of children in climbing them. Taro Yashima, whose real name is Jun Iwamatsu, in his rhythmic telling of the story of little Momo in *Umbrella* (1958) showed a sympathetic feeling for childhood and its universal pride in a new rain outfit as he described the long wait for rain by the little Japanese girl in New York. The same sympathy and understanding characterized his story of the final triumph of *Crow Boy* (1955), the inarticulate boy in a Japanese school.

Robert McCloskey's *One Morning in Maine* (1952) combined joy in the beauties of the Maine coast with the drama of the loss of a front tooth. His *Time of Wonder* (1957), with its beautiful water colors of the same region, won him the Caldecott Award for the second time in 1958. Since

he had won the award before, the committee's decision had to be unanimous, making this perhaps the greatest recognition which can come to an artist-author.

Perhaps at the top of the list, so far as the children were concerned, in childlike quality, in sense of place, in delightful humor, and in dramatic climax was Lynd Ward's *The Biggest Bear* (1952), which, in its unique vitality of both story and pictures, presents a most satisfying unity of effect.

From *The Biggest Bear* by Lynd Ward. Il. by author. Houghton, 1952.

Fortunately for children, a vein of humor and hilarity ran through many of the picture books of the fifties. It began with the irresistible nonsense of Dr. Seuss's *If I Ran the Zoo* (1950) and the comic book antics of Hans A. Rey's *Curious George Rides a Bike* (1952), and it ended with another uproarious pair, Sesyle Joslin's *What Do You Say, Dear?* (1958) and Gene Zion's *No*

I beg your pardon.

From *What Do You Say, Dear?* by Sesyle Joslin. Il. by Maurice Sendak. Young Scott Books, 1958.

Roses for Harry! (1958). Accompanied by the ridiculous and highly imaginative pictures of Maurice Sendak, the incidents of *What Do You Say, Dear?* teach animal babies to mind their manners in ludicrous settings which have implications for children. The resentment of the little dog in *No Roses for Harry!* against the yellow roses in his winter jacket is not only justified but vindicated when, in the end, he loosens a stitch and releases a thread, the end of which an accommodating bird carries up into a tree for a woolly lining for its nest. Harry's delight knows no bounds as his rose-trimmed knitted jacket vanishes into space.

In between came Benjamin Elkin's *The Loudest Noise in the World* (1954) with vigorous James Daugherty illustrations and Louise Fatio's most buoyant and engaging happy lion (*The Happy Lion*, 1954), who, finding the door to his cage open, goes gaily into town to return the calls of the friends who have visited him in the zoo. This is the

kind of obvious incongruity which little children can appreciate.

Eve Titus's clever little mouse, Anatole, the cheese-taster in a factory, is equally original and humorous in *Anatole* (1956) and in *Anatole and the Cat* (1957). In the latter, the children's previous knowledge of "belling the cat" helps them to enter with glee into Anatole's success. It combines good storytelling with successful integration of text and pictures.

The variety and experimentation with new themes which characterize the picture books of this decade are well illustrated by four which are especially original. Marie Ets's *Play with Me* (1955), the story of a little

From *Play with Me* by Marie Ets. Il. by author. Viking, 1955.

girl who learns that the animals of the wood will come to her if she sits quietly, is a triumph in the sympathetic revelation of a child and of animals. It is hailed by artists for its feeling for composition, its unique sense of quiet, and its mood of magic. With originality and imaginative use of color and design, Ann and Paul Rand in *Sparkle and Spin* (1957) have given young children a sense of the beauty, the music, and the fun of words. *Elf Owl* (1958) by Mary and Conrad Buff reveals the drama of animal life in the desert through the eyes of two little elf owls sitting quietly in a cactus bush. Finally, Joan Walsh Anglund in *A Friend Is Someone Who Likes You* (1958), with delicate little pictures of good times and personal relationships, makes concrete for little children the satisfactions of friendship. In childlike fashion, she develops through examples at the child's own level a concept or generalization—a technique which several authors have attempted in recent years.

THE INFLUENCE OF FOREIGN ARTISTS AND SETTINGS

Foreign settings and artists have made distant lands real to little children in the picture books of this decade. Selina Chönz's *A Bell for Ursli* (1950), with its delightful lithographs, tells the story of a Swiss child's trip through the snow to his mountain cabin for his cowbell. With it he led the procession of children to whom spring brought the opportunity to take the cattle to the mountain top for summer grazing. The setting is Swiss, but the desire to be the leader is universal. Seignobosc (pseud. Françoise) during this decade presented Jeanne-Marie in two beautiful picture books in which she counts her sheep (*Jeanne-Marie Counts Her Sheep*, 1951) and goes to Paris (*Jeanne-Marie in Gay Paris*, 1956). In 1957 Bettina Ehrlich added *Pantaloni* to her charming and colorful picture books of Italian village life. It is the very human story of a little boy's search for his lost dog.

After World War II children's writers again turned to the revelation of life in other countries. Ann Nolan Clark found in Guatemala and Latin America two distinguished native boys who were true to the heritage of their ancient peoples: Cusi, the boy herder of the sacred Inca llamas in the wild mountains of Peru, whose story is poetically told in *Secret of the Andes* (1952), and Santiago (*Santiago*, 1955), the Guatemalan boy who renounces a privileged Spanish home to teach his own people. Interpretations such as Ann Nolan Clark's have helped the modern child who is sensitive and a gifted reader to recognize the values in cultures older and in some cases more primitive than his own.

Meindert De Jong's powerful and dramatic story, *The Wheel on the School* (1954), brought to young readers in America the drama of a group of Dutch children who put a wheel on the chimney of their school to attract storks for good luck. What a storm at sea can mean to the people and animals of Holland is vividly and dramatically portrayed. Two years later in *The House of Sixty Fathers* (1956) he gave to American boys and girls some notion of the tragedy of the Chinese children who were separated from their parents in their attempted escape from Japanese conquerors. In Belle Rugh's *Crystal Mountain* (1955) middle grade children share in the mystery, the adventure, and the understanding of Arab life and background which came to a group of American boys and their English playmate in a visit to Lebanon.

In 1956 Eleanor Lattimore brought out for younger readers who were old friends of the lively little Chinese boy, *Little Pear and the Rabbits*, with a country fair in which he acquired his pets. At the same time, Dorothy Rhoads presented a slowly moving story of a Mayan Indian boy, who, during his father's illness, planted and saved the harvest until the rains came (*The Corn Grows Ripe*, 1956). The illustrations are full of the heavy spectacular foliage of Yucatan. David Fletcher's *Confetti for Corticelli* (1957) revealed the joys of the Mardi Gras in Sicily.

Phyllis Krasilovsky's *The Cow Who Fell in the Canal* (1957) makes her ludicrous tumble the occasion for drifting down the canal on a raft to admire the beauties of the Dutch setting. The colorful and clearly drawn pictures are a delight to children. Marcia Brown sets in Venice her picture book of *Felice* (1958), the cat adopted by a gondolier's son. It is full of the atmosphere of Venice and the shimmering colors of the canals. None of the picture books of foreign places has been more beloved than *Nine Days to Christmas* (1959) by Marie Ets and Aurora Labastida. It is a charming and colorful Christmas story of a Mexican kindergarten child and her first posada celebration. A major value of this picture book lies in the fact that the heroine belongs to an upper class Mexican family, a group seldom pictured in children's books.

Especially distinctive among similar books for older children was Natalie Carlson's *The Family under the Bridge* (1958) on the Seine in Paris with their friend and benefactor, Arnaud, whose two greatest dislikes in life had been children and work. Eventually he took on both and enjoyed the combination. Mrs. Carlson's *Happy Orpheline* stories, *The Happy Orpheline* (1957) and *A Brother for the Orphelines* (1959), dispelled the long faces which had hitherto been associated with orphanages. Edith Unnerstad brought a touch of Sweden to American boys and girls in her sympathetic account of *The Spettecake Holiday* (1958) in which a little boy spends some months on his grandmother's Stubba farm while his mother is ill. The grand climax comes when he carries home a spettecake for the doctor who cured her.

Francis Kalnay described the exciting life of a would-be gaucho in the pampas (*Chucaro, Wild Pony of the Pampas*, 1958) much to the delight of upper grade boys. Finally, Paul Berna's *The Horse without a Head* came from France in 1958 to make the gangs of children in an underprivileged neighborhood near Paris real to American readers as they found adventure and mystery in a toy wooden horse, iron-wheeled and headless.

Fritz Eichenberg and Hans Fischer, along with Maurice Sendak, an American of foreign parentage, demonstrated once more in this decade what the American picture book owes to foreign influences. Eichenberg's *Ape in a Cape* (1952) introduces a new imaginative concept into his alphabet. It is not enough to have *H for Hare*, but *H*

for Hare at the fair, and not merely *I for Irish setter,* but *I* for an *Irish setter with a letter.* Both pictures and rhymes add a new imaginative quality to the letter-picture relationships. Hans Fischer introduced a new playful quality into his *Pitschi, the Kitten Who Always Wanted to Be Something Else* (1953) and into his strikingly original picture story, *The Birthday* (1954). The re-

From *Pitschi* by Hans Fischer. Il. by author. Harcourt, 1948.

markable flexibility in Maurice Sendak's talent for illustration is demonstrated in the contrast between his highly imaginative and beautiful pictures of the magic of moonlight in Janice M. Udry's *The Moon Jumpers* (1959) and the equally delicate sketches of Else H. Minarik's *Little Bear* (1957) and *Father Bear Comes Home* (1959). In the latter, no matter how simple the drawings, each character, in spite of changes in mood and manner, becomes a personality in his own right.

THE CHILDREN OF THE UNITED STATES IN BOOKS

American children of various regions and

Hare at the fair

From *Ape in a Cape* by Fritz Eichenberg. Il. by author. Harcourt, 1952.

nationalities appear in several distinguished books of this decade. First, Joseph Krumgold won the Newbery Award for his sincere and dignified story of Miguel, the twelve-year-old New Mexican boy for whom growing up was symbolized by the right to accompany the sheep herders to the upland summer pasture in the Sangre de Cristo mountains (. . . *And Now Miguel,* 1953). The story is slow-moving because life is slow for Miguel himself, but its insights into human personality and family relations in a New Mexican mountain village are well worth the effort to read it. The illustrations by Jean Charlot are in perfect keeping with the story.

From *Little Bear* by Else H. Minarik.
Il. by Maurice Sendak. Harper, 1957.

Two years later Jennie D. Lindquist brought out her charming book called *The Golden Name Day* (1955), which shows how a little American girl shared the celebrations of a Swedish family and herself achieved a golden name day in the end. A similar understanding of Amish children and their backgrounds in Pennsylvania comes to boys and girls from Virginia Sorensen's sensitive revelation of the fears of her Plain Girl (*Plain Girl,* 1955) as she faced attending a public school.

MORE REAL BOYS AND GIRLS

Fiction for the middle years has much less depth during this decade than in the previous one although a number of good stories were brought out. For younger children Carolyn Haywood's Betsy continued her popular daily doings in summer and in winter (*Betsy's Busy Summer,* 1956, and *Betsy's Winterhouse,* 1958), and Eddie made music in a hilarious school and family story in which he became "a vocalist" with the orchestra (*Eddie Makes Music,* 1957). Most hilarious of all, Keith Robertson's Henry Reed achieved fame in Princeton, that most scientifically minded of New Jersey towns, by the unexpected results of his summer's experiments. In the end, he even deigned to paint an *Inc.* after his firm name on the barn in tardy and reluctant recognition of the part played in his success by a mere girl (*Henry Reed, Inc.,* 1958). The story represents the height of inventiveness, suggestive characterization, and hilarious humor for both boys and girls. Robert McCloskey's illustrations match those he did for *Homer Price* (1943).

Beverly Cleary's Henry Huggins (*Henry Huggins,* 1950) comes out victorious from the many unpredictable difficulties in a real boy's life, including his adventures with his friend, Beezus (Beatrice) (*Henry and Beezus,* 1952), and with his dog, Ribsy (*Henry and Ribsy,* 1954). In 1957 he secures a paper route through the unexpected intervention of Ramona, Beezus's ubiquitous little sister (*Henry and the Paper Route,* 1957). Every third grade boy will find himself in these simply written stories to be read for sheer fun.

Old Yeller (1956) by Frederick B. Gipson has given older boys a sympathetic picture of the love of a boy for a dog, the understanding which developed between them on the ranch, and the poignancy of their separation in the end, an experience which plays a part in the boy's growing up. Beverly Cleary's *The Luckiest Girl* (1958) has proved that the author can write a distinctive junior novel to the great satisfaction of adolescent girls.

IMAGINATIVE STORIES FOR CHILDREN

The early 1950's were rich in imaginative stories for children. Younger boys and girls delighted in the ingenuity of Alice Dalgliesh's small boy who not only proved that there were *Bears on Hemlock Mountain* (1952), but foiled them by his own cleverness. Virginia Kahl put a touch of Old Austria into her *Away Went Wolfgang!*

(1954) and delighted children by her humorously rhymed tale of the *The Duchess Bakes a Cake* (1955), a cake so light that she sat on it to keep it from rising. Rise it did, however, with her on it, so that her friends had to eat their way up to rescue her as she ate her way down!

Middle grade children thrilled to the sprightly humor of Ellen MacGregor's *Miss Pickerell Goes to Mars* (1951), which gave them a bit of science fiction of their very own. Two fantasies that topped the list for them were E. B. White's *Charlotte's Web*

From *Charlotte's Web* by E. B. White. Il. by Garth Williams. Harper, 1952.

(1952) and Mary Norton's *The Borrowers* (1953). Both were original in conception, with a touch of magic, a rhythmic and imaginative style, and a feeling for characterization. Charlotte, the spider, and her philosophical concern for the troubled pig, Wilbur, and Mary Norton's little creatures no taller than a pencil (*The Borrowers*, 1953), who miraculously inhabited the secret places of the old English country house, have already won a permanent place in literature for children. Imaginative readers have likewise taken to their hearts Lucy M. Boston's *The Children of Green Knowe* (1955), in which, in the absence of other playmates, lonely Tolly conjures up the boys and girls of his great-grandmother's storybook world.

The retelling of old tales and the writing of new ones flourished during these years. The decade began with the republication in 1950 of the *Arthur Rackham Fairy Book,* which helped preserve the imaginative pictures of an artist particularly skilled in penetrating the unseen. Dorothy Hosford did her distinguished *Thunder of the Gods* (1952), the story of the heroes of Asgard presented with vigor in both pictures and style.

In 1952 Natalie Carlson, with her delightful sense of humor and lightness of touch, added to these collections *The Talking Cat and Other Stories of French Canada.* Joice NanKivell produced *Tales of Christophilos* (1954), which combined imagination and legendary lore with the story of a little goatherd in a Greek village after World

From *The Borrowers* by Mary Norton. Il. by Beth and Joe Krush. Harcourt, 1953.

War II. Philip Sherlock brought to life the Jamaican tales of *Anansi, the Spider Man* (1954) with strikingly interpretive pictures by Marcia Brown. Next came Lucia Borski and Kate B. Miller with a reissue of an old collection of Polish stories in *The Jolly Tailor and Other Fairy Tales* (1957).

Especially welcome was the reappearance of Ella Young's dramatic retelling of the famous old Irish cycle of *The Wonder Smith and His Son* (1957) and her own tale of *The Unicorn with the Silver Shoes* (1957), a story full of the beauty and wonder of Irish faerie lore. Harold Courlander continued to add to "the tongues speaking to our children" in *The Hat-Shaking Dance and Other Tales from the Gold Coast* (1957) and *The Tiger's Whisker and Other Tales and Legends of Asia and the Pacific* (1959). At the same time, tall tales of boisterous American heroes abounded in Ellis Credle's delightful stories of the Carolina Blue Ridge, called *Tall Tales from the High Hills and Other Stories* (1957), in James Bowman's *Mike Fink* (1957), and in Harold W. Felton's *New Tall Tales of Pecos Bill* (1958). Katherine Love brought out a much needed new collection of Parker Fillmore's tales of Finland and Czechoslovakia in *The Shepherd's Nosegay* (1958), selected from three previous volumes then out of print.

Nor were the old favorites for little children forgotten during this decade. Ruth Sawyer retold the story of *Journey Cake, Ho!* (1953) accompanied by rollicking pictures by Robert McCloskey in which Johnny fairly leaps from the page. Putnam supplied a brief text in English to accompany the ancient Japanese scroll by Toba Sojo, called *The Animal Frolic* (1954). A striking richness of color and sureness of line characterized Antonio Frasconi's pictures for *See and Say* (1955), an illustrated vocabulary

in Italian, French, Spanish, and English. He also did woodcuts in color and black and white for *The House That Jack Built; La Maison Que Jacques A Batie* (1958). In keeping with the recent trend toward teaching foreign languages in the elementary school, the narrative is rhythmically told in both French and English on double-page spreads.

John Langstaff contributed two picture books of the musical old rhymes, *Frog Went A-Courtin'* (1955) and *Over in the Meadow* (1957), with pictures as colorful and as delightful in humorous detail as an

From *Frog Went A-Courtin'* by John Langstaff. Il. by Feodor Rojankovsky. Harcourt, 1955.

artist could create. Barbara Cooney won the Caldecott Award for her exquisite drawings done in brilliant color and her medieval designs for a retelling of Chaucer's *Chanticleer and the Fox* (1958).

From *Chanticleer and the Fox* by Geoffrey Chaucer. Il. by Barbara Cooney. Thomas Y. Crowell, 1958.

At the same time excellent versions of individual favorites among the fairy tales continued to appear, with new illustrations. Marcia Brown's *Dick Whittington and His Cat* (1950), *Cinderella* (1954), *The Flying Carpet* (1956), and *The Three Billy Goats Gruff* (1957) all seem equally authentic

From *The Three Billy Goats Gruff* by P. C. Asbjörnsen and J. E. Moe. Il. by Marcia Brown. Harcourt, 1957.

whether she is picturing the bold stride of Dick Whittington in fourteenth century London, the gay ball of *Cinderella,* the brilliant colors and Oriental motifs in the *Flying Carpet* of *The Arabian Nights*, or the eerie troll of Norway's fjord country. In 1958 Phyllis Fenner, on the basis of her experience as a storyteller in the Manhassett Public Schools in New York, made a particularly felicitous selection of nursery and folk tales for the primary grades in a beautifully illustrated volume called *Mostly Magic* (1958). It is the first book of *Through Golden Windows* (1958), a ten-volume anthology of readings for elementary school children which may be purchased singly or in sets.

Erik Blegvad, translating and illustrating Andersen's *The Swineherd* (1958), entered into the spirit of the original in his rhythmic language and old-fashioned Danish pictures, and Hans Fischer brought new life to Charles Perrault's *Puss in Boots* (1959) with

From *Puss in Boots* by Charles Perrault. Il. by Hans Fischer. Harcourt, 1959.

his sure and brilliant colors and his graphic lines. The last decade has combined the promise of the picture book of the 1930's with a wealth of experiments by new and able artists and writers, all of which augur well for the future.

POETRY AGAIN

Poetry, new and old, flourished in the 1950's. Harold Behn appeared on the scene in 1949 and again in the fifties with his lyric genius and his ability to see through the eyes of a child. Both qualities found immediate acceptance in his *The Little Hill* (1949), his *Windy Morning* (1953), and his *Wizard*

in the Well (1956). Little children delighted in Marguerite de Angeli's *Book of Nursery and Mother Goose Rhymes* (1954) from

From *Book of Nursery and Mother Goose Rhymes* by Marguerite de Angeli. Il. by author. Doubleday, 1954.

the moment it appeared with its generous-sized pages and its delicately toned pictures, full of the everyday joys and sorrows of childhood, as old and as new-fashioned as the Mother Goose rhymes themselves. Katherine Lines's *Lavender's Blue* (1954), though somewhat unconventional in some of its choices and versions, presented a gay and yet delicately old-fashioned picture book of Mother Goose and folk rhymes.

William Jay Smith's hilarious nonsense in *Laughing Time* (1955) and *Boy Blue's Book of Beasts* (1957) gave support to Samuel McChord Crothers's contention that poetry and "great joyous laughter" should go hand in hand.[168] So also did William Cole's popular collection, *Humorous Poetry for Children* (1955), which was followed later by *I Went to the Animal Fair* (1958) with its rhythmical nonsense and clever drawings. Katherine Love's *A Little Laughter* (1957) served the same purpose for somewhat older readers.

Three distinguished compilations of poetry for older children of special talent have appeared during the 1950's. One is Herbert Read's *This Way, Delight* (1956), a careful selection of traditional verse accompanied by a delightful chapter on "What Is Poetry?" The others are by Helen Plotz, who, with originality and imagination aided by a distinguished format, has prepared two striking volumes of verse for pupils with special gifts—one on science and mathematics called *Imagination's Other Place* (1955) and one on music and art entitled *Untune the Sky* (1957). Standards in selection of the poems in these volumes are high, and the illustrations have sufficient dignity and spirit to appeal to the superior readers for whom the poems were chosen.

Helen Ferris revealed her intimate knowledge of young readers and of poetry in *Favorite Poems, Old and New* (1957), an omnibus collection offering a broad range of poems about a wide variety of subjects. It has already proved its usefulness in schools and libraries and its popularity with children. Although May Hill Arbuthnot's *Time for Poetry* (1951, revised 1959) is addressed to teachers rather than to children, it seems impossible to omit so delightful an anthology from this list. The title came from the frequent response of teachers to Mrs. Arbuthnot's question of the place of poetry in the elementary school. They had "no time for poetry." With the help of this fresh and stimulating volume and the generous and understanding treatment of poetry in her *Children and Books* (1957), surely there can be no further response of this kind to her contagious enthusiasm for poetry and for children.

Several old favorites have appeared in new format, notably A. A. Milne's *When We Were Very Young* and *Now We Are Six* in a large, attractive volume called *The World of Christopher Robin* (1958), which contains eight new illustrations in color. The children's favorite poems by individual poets have also appeared in new collections which will be especially useful in schools and libraries—the most distinguished being *You Come Too; Favorite Poems of Robert Frost for Young Readers* (1959).

HISTORY IN FICTION

During the last decade, much fiction, especially for older children, has been historical in setting. As has already been indicated, in 1953 a complete new edition of Laura Ingalls Wilder's *Little House* series came from the press with delightfully warm, homelike illustrations by Garth Williams. Alice Dalgliesh, in *The Courage of Sarah Noble* (1954), the story of a little girl's heroism in early Connecticut, where she learned to know the

Indians as friends, gave younger boys and girls satisfaction in discovering that children their age had a part in settling the wilderness. Robert Lawson's *The Great Wheel* (1957), with its touch of humor and striking black and white drawings, reveals in the life of the Irish boy immigrant the part played by European workers in building our nation. Children are especially interested in his helping to construct the ferris wheel at the Columbian Exposition in Chicago in 1893.

The last three years of the decade brought from the press four distinguished junior novels with carefully drawn historical backgrounds. Harold Keith's *Rifles for Watie* (1957) and William O. Steele's *The Perilous Road* (1958) center in the Civil War. The first is the dramatic story of a young farm boy's years as a scout with the Union forces in the West, where he becomes involved in the intricacies of Cherokee fighting both on their own behalf and in the war between the states. *The Perilous Road*, deftly told with a touch of philosophy, has at its heart a young boy's questionings concerning the senselessness of war while at the same time he greatly admires true courage.

A similar theme runs through Mari Sandoz's treatment of the peace-loving Cheyenne who braves the anger of the tribe to become a tamer of wild horses rather than a seeker after scalps. *The Horsecatcher* (1957) is a book full of deep insight and excellent character portrayal.

Girls found in Elizabeth Speare's *The Witch of Blackbird Pond* (1958) a remark-able combination of rich historical background with three adolescent love affairs, a dashing hero, and a heroine to match. Yet the general tone is serious, and the revelation of Puritan thought and mode of living is unsurpassed in fiction for the average adolescent reader.

THE EXPANSION OF BIOGRAPHY FOR ALL AGES

In the field of biography in particular, it is important to have the stories of our national heroes told at many levels of maturity and of difficulty so that pupils of all ages and of varied intellectual power may be able to read and enjoy them. The decade from 1950 to 1960 added significantly to the progress already made in the forties. The Aulaires continued their earlier series of picture story biographies with a very popular *Buffalo*

From *The Witch of Blackbird Pond* by Elizabeth George Speare.
Il. by author. Houghton, 1958.

Bill (1952) and an equally usable *Columbus* (1955). In her *Ride on the*

From *Columbus* by Ingri and Edgar Parin D' Aulaire. Il. by authors. Doubleday, 1955.

Wind (1956), a biography distinguished for both pictures and text, Alice Dalgliesh presented for middle elementary grade pupils Lindbergh's boyhood desire to be an aviator and the drama of his nonstop solo flight to Paris.

In 1953, Robert Lawson in the same humorous spirit in which he had earlier presented Ben Franklin through the eyes of his good mouse, Amos (*Ben and Me,* 1939), gave somewhat older readers Paul Revere as seen by his horse (*Mr. Revere and I,* 1953). The conversion of the horse from aristocratic to democratic sympathies adds much humor and drama to the story.

Genevieve Foster wrote her biographies, *Abraham Lincoln* and *Andrew Jackson,* in 1950 and 1951, slender volumes which combine dignity of text and pictures with her recognized skill in infusing facts with life. Such books are as useful for older pupils who read at a level below that of their general maturity as they are with fourth grade children. Henry Steele Commager contributed his recognized historical scholarship to *America's Robert E. Lee* (1951). The significance of the word *America* in the title shows the regard of the author for men on both sides of the war between the states. During this decade also May McNeer and Lynd Ward cooperated in the biographies of John Wesley (*John Wesley,* 1951) and Martin Luther (*Martin Luther,* 1953), volumes known especially for their colorful and dignified pictures by Lynd Ward. The same year they presented in *Armed with Courage* (1957) needed short biographies of men and women of spiritual courage like Gandhi, Schweitzer, Jane Addams, and Wilfred Grenfell. In 1957 May McNeer brought out *America's Abraham Lincoln,* again with illustrations by Lynd Ward. Distinguished for its delightful style, its use of sources, and its colorful sketches by Rojankovsky is Esther Averill's new edition of her earlier *The Voyages of Jacques Cartier*, now called *Cartier Sails the St. Lawrence* (1956). Upper elementary school girls also delighted in Ruth Franchere's *Willa* (1958), the charming story of the childhood of Willa Cather in early Nebraska.

For older children the decade opened with two significant biographies of the spirit —*Amos Fortune, Free Man* (1950) by Elizabeth Yates and *Gandhi, Fighter without a Sword* (1950) by Jeanette Eaton. After the vivid scene of the slave traders' closing in on the harvest festival of the Negroes in Africa, Amos Fortune finds himself chained beneath the hatches of a slave ship turned toward America. "He compelled himself to remember as far back as he could in the past that he might have something far more than his body to carry into the future."[169] The story of his life in New England, first as a slave and later as a free man, is sympathetically and beautifully told by the author. *Gandhi, Fighter without a Sword* is more than the life of a great leader. It is an interpretation of India, its aspirations and its problems.

In 1950 also came Clara Ingram Judson's *Abraham Lincoln, Friend of the People* (1950), the first of a series of biographies which in 1960 won her the Laura Ingalls Wilder Award. Her vision of the warp and woof of America conceived of its great leaders as the warp of a noble design holding firm the strands through which people from all nations wove in and out to give it strength and character. Her Lincoln was followed by *George Washington, Leader of the People* (1951), by *Thomas Jefferson, Champion of the People* (1952), by *Theodore Roosevelt, Fighting Patriot* (1953), by *Andrew Jackson, Frontier Statesman* (1954), and by *Mr. Justice Holmes* in 1956 and *Benjamin Franklin* in 1957.

Her care in research was recognized everywhere and her understanding both of what boys and girls wanted to know about their country's leaders and what they should know. Her characters emerged real and alive because of her intimate search for the incidents which revealed them. She believed that for the upper elementary and junior high school pupils authentic, colorful, and interesting pictures were important—pictures that would interpret as well as illustrate. Her humorous experience with the boy who liked George Washington but couldn't understand "why he married that old lady" led to her search for the charming picture of Martha Washington coming down stairs as a bride minus the white hair and cap in which she has been wont to appear in children's books. Kodachromes of the Lincoln dioramas of the Chicago Historical Society make her volume on Lincoln unique.

Sterling North's *Abe Lincoln, Log Cabin to White House* (1956) has proved especially useful, also, for average readers in the seventh and eighth grades.

James Daugherty, in 1953, produced his *Marcus and Narcissa Whitman, Pioneers of*

Oregon in which he combined both the spiritual and physical struggles of the early band of missionaries to the Oregon Indians. Again, his virile and at the same time spiritually charged pictures of the pioneer days lent distinction to the book.

In 1955 Jean Latham introduced her *Carry On, Mr. Bowditch,* a remarkable combination of the rich background of ships and sea in early New England and the growth of a young boy from apprentice to mathematician, astronomer, and navigator. Her *Young Man in a Hurry; the Story of Cyrus W. Field* (1958) opened up new interests for older boys and girls—both the laying of the Atlantic cable and the area of business.

The unusual variety in excellent biographies for older pupils which appeared during the decade 1950 to 1960 is well illustrated by four which followed in 1957 and 1958—Emma G. Sterne's *Mary McLeod Bethune* (1957), the story of the Negro girl who became an educational leader among her people; Jeanette Eaton's *America's Own Mark Twain* (1958); Rafaello Busoni's *The Man Who Was Don Quixote* (1958); and Douglas S. Freeman's *Lee of Virginia* (1958). There is still need, however, for more good biographies of women and more simple biographies for children in areas other than the lives of the early patriots.

INFORMATIVE BOOKS IN HISTORY AND GEOGRAPHY

Although informative books in the social studies have in general given way during the fifties before the upsurge of interest in science, certain authors have contributed significantly to the children's knowledge of American backgrounds. Elizabeth Baity has added materially to the children's understanding of the Indian by her *Americans before Columbus* (1951) with its striking illustrations by C. B. Falls. Samuel E. Morison has deepened their appreciation of the life and purposes of our founding fathers in the illuminating details of *The Story of the "Old Colony" of New Plymouth (1620-1692)* (1956). Harold Coy in 1958 brought out *The Americans,* intended, he says, "to increase the enjoyment of reading about American history by showing how Americans lived, how they felt, and how they tackled new problems in good times and stormy weather."[170] It bids fair to succeed in its useful purpose. Genevieve Foster has added to her original and scholarly horizontal study of history *The World of Captain John Smith, 1580-1631* (1959).

Three oversized books of this period show clearly what profuse illustrations, charts and diagrams, and plenty of space can do to make historical material clear and appealing. They are Edwin Tunis's books on *Colonial Living* (1957) and on *Indians* (1959) before the white man, and Margaret Mead's *People and Places* (1959), an introduction to anthropology for children which makes principles and details clear through striking drawings and photographs.

Gerald W. Johnson has completed a new dramatic trilogy giving the full sweep of

America's history in books addressed to Peter, to whom he wishes to make his country's story vivid and personal: *America Is Born* (1959); *America Grows Up* (1960); and *America Moves Forward* (1961). A more informal approach to Indian life has come to middle grade readers through the work of Robert Hofsinde, who writes out of his own experience. Especially popular is his *Indian Sign Language* (1956). May McNeer and Lynd Ward have met the needs of the same readers in *The California Gold Rush* (1950).

In keeping with the desire to illuminate topics of current interest is Harry B. Ellis's authentic and detailed story of *The Arabs* (1958). May McNeer produced in 1953 *The Mexican Story,* full of the gripping pageantry of Mexican history, and in 1958 *The Canadian Story,* a swiftly moving, episodic account of the history of Canada. The handsome lithographs in both books are by Lynd Ward.

It is a notable fact that in most of these historical materials there is a continued trend away from the story of wars and battles toward a deeper understanding of cultural and anthropological trends and a tracing of the influences from times past which condition life in our world today. At the same time, books like Richard B. Morris's *The First Book of the Constitution* (1958) and Harold Coy's *The First Book of the Supreme Court* (1958) have given children needed information, in language they can understand, concerning the circumstances of the

making of our constitution and government and the vital function of both in contemporary life.

Little children also share this re-creation of the early days of American life and their meaning for our country today. Alice Dalgliesh in *The Thanksgiving Story* (1954), an account of the Pilgrims from the sailing of the Mayflower to the Thanksgiving feast, has created a dramatic and dignified story, the significance of which she succeeds in

From *The Thanksgiving Story* by Alice Dalgliesh. Il. by Helen Sewell. Scribner, 1954. ©1954 Alice Dalgliesh and Helen Sewell.

making real to little children. The effect of climax is greatly enhanced by the clear, bold pictures of Helen Sewell, whose shifting color scheme helps to accentuate the mood of the narrative. In *The Fourth of July Story* (1956) Miss Dalgliesh presents in colorful illustrations and dignified text the meaning of the Declaration of Independence and the solemnity of the occasion of its adoption by the Continental Congress. In pictures and in words she succeeds in making the message of the famous document concrete. Another social studies book of great value for little children is Dahlov Ipcar's *Ten Big Farms* (1958). Within the framework of a family search for a new home in the country, the author presents a striking array of farms in simple text and colorful double-page spreads.

Weisgard flourished. Perhaps this is because the major emphasis in the 1950's was upon topics too mature for little children to understand. Franklyn M. Branley, however, an astronomer at the American Museum-Hayden Planetarium, attempted *A Book of Satellites for You* (1958), which explains with vivid illustrations for primary grade children the scientific purpose and method of launching satellites.

For middle grade children scientific writing on a variety of topics increased notably during this decade. Lynd Ward, in his discussion of the book artist from 1946-56, selects for special commendation Herman and Nina Schneider's *You among the Stars* (1951) because of the sense of beauty and wonder achieved by Symeon Schimin in the illustrations.[171] Hans A. Rey in 1954 produced *Find the Constellations,* a prac-

From *Ten Big Farms* by Dahlov Ipcar. Il. by author. Knopf, 1958.

THE BOOM IN SCIENCE

Science books for little children did not achieve at this time the stature of those of the 1940's when handsome picture books with distinguished text and illustrations by artists like Roger Duvoisin and Leonard

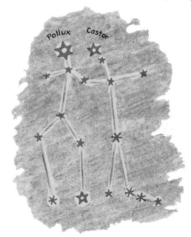

From *Find the Constellations* by H. A. Rey. Il. by author. Houghton, 1954.

tical handbook with excellent charts and maps. Space travel was included in it. John Lewellen's *The Earth Satellite* (1957) also helped to satisfy the curiosity of middle grade children, aroused during the events of the International Geophysical Year.

As early as 1950 Henry Billings had introduced into his *Diesel-Electric 4030* a combined sense of precision and beauty in the picturing of machinery. His graphic description of the workings of a diesel engine as seen from the cab of the locomotive in which he made the run from New York to Albany equalled in interest the skillfully drawn pictures and diagrams. Jerome S.

From *Diesel-Electric 4030* by Henry Billings. Il. by author. Viking, 1956.

Meyer in his *Machines* (1958) gave middle grade boys the information they were waiting for concerning the evolution of machines from scissors to steam shovels.

Fascinating information on many other aspects of nature and animal life was also made available to children of the intermediate grades. Only a few illustrative titles and authors can be mentioned here. Maribelle Cormack's *The First Book of Stones* has been a favorite ever since it appeared in 1950. Addison Webb's *Song of the Seasons* (1950), which is both interesting and informative, guides children's study of birds and animals throughout the year. Professor Herbert S. Zim's invaluable contribution to intermediate grade science still continued. His *Frogs and Toads* (1950) and his *Alligators and Crocodiles* (1952) are among the most read of his recent contributions although his guides to stars, to rocks and minerals, and the like continue to fulfill an important function in the schools. Of these, *Reptiles and Amphibians* (1956), which he did with Hobart M. Smith, is one of the most useful. Albert Tibbetts's *The First Book of Bees* (1952) has been deservedly popular. Herman Schneider's *Everyday Weather and How It Works* (1951) tells boys and girls what they want to know about familiar phenomena while Zolotow's *The Storm Book* (1952) dramatizes with striking pictures a phenomenon which often fills children with awe and fear, giving it a scientific foundation. Roy C. Andrews's *All about Dinosaurs* (1953) is one of the most useful of the *All-about* books. Another valuable addition to the science collection is Carroll L. Fenton's *Prehistoric World* (1954).

Thelma H. Bell's delightful treatment of snow (*Snow*, 1954) both in text and in accurate, artistic, and delicately colored designs, combines the wonder and the beauty

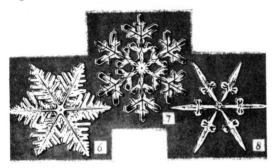

From *Snow* by Thelma H. Bell.
Il. by Corydon Bell. Viking, 1954.

of snow with information concerning its composition and its effects upon the life of men, women, and children. Glenn O. Blough has furnished many simple and accurate descriptions of scientific events adapted to the needs and understanding of early elementary school children. Typical is his *Wait for the Sunshine; the Story of Seasons and Growing Things* (1954). Millicent Selsam has made a needed contribution in such titles as *Play with Seeds* (1957), which combines suggestions for experimentation with an explanation of the importance of seeds for food, clothing, and other manufactured products. Elizabeth K. Cooper's *Science in Your Own Back Yard* (1958), by guiding the older child's observation of scientific phenomena in his own back yard, stimulates simple experimentation in astronomy, botany, geology, and zoology. And

finally, Will Barker's *Winter-Sleeping Wildlife* (1958) has added depth and understanding to the older children's curiosity concerning hibernation among animals.

The most significant contribution in scientific materials for children has been made during this decade in books for older boys and girls. At least three of these are oversized books with illuminating drawings and compelling illustrations which may also be used with better readers in the intermediate grades. One of these is *Prehistoric Animals* (1954) by William E. Scheele, director of the Cleveland Museum of Natural History. Man's growing control over the forces of nature is the subject of Lancelot Hogben's *The Wonderful World of Energy* (1957). Its graphic illustrations and effective diagrams capture children's imagination and give them the information they seek. Another book is Rachel Carson's *The Sea around Us* (1958), which has been adapted from her earlier definitive work on the subject. Its colorful illustrations coupled with

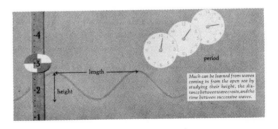

From *The Sea around Us* by Rachel Carson.
Il. by Rene Martin, maps by Emil Lowenstein.
©1958 Golden Press, Inc.

From *The Sea around Us* by Rachel Carson.
Il. by Rene Martin, maps by Emil Lowenstein.
©1958 Golden Press, Inc.

a wealth of interesting information make it indispensable for the children's library. It is useful in both the intermediate and upper grades.

Most important of all to older boys and girls has been the mystery of the new explorations of the universe made possible by the launching of satellites and the sending of men into space. An Athens newspaper the night after Colonel John Glenn's flight carried the heading: "Colonel Glenn has been further from the earth than any man living and closer to the hearts of its people." Small wonder that boys and girls have sought background information about such significant events! Roy A. Gallant has done a series of readable books on *Exploring the Universe* (1956), *Exploring the Planets* (1958), and *Exploring the Sun* (1958). They combine historical background with

clear and interesting scientific discussions as well as with effective and often dramatic illustrations.

Franklyn M. Branley, in *Exploring by Satellite* (1957), told the story of the Project Vanguard, giving details of the construction of the satellite, the scientific principles and instruments underlying its operation, and the evidence it might be expected to gather. His *The Nine Planets* (1958) pleased scientists and book-makers alike by its simple, clear presentation of the characteristics of the planets and the contributions of various astronomers to man's knowledge of them.

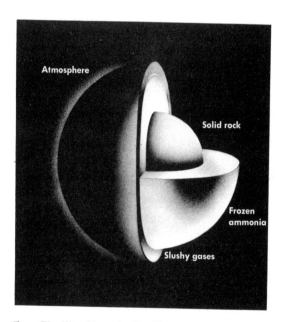

From *The Nine Planets* by Franklyn M. Branley.
Il. by Helmut K. Wimmer. Thomas Y. Crowell, 1958.

Plans for the International Geophysical Year and interest in map-making in general gave unusual timeliness to Beulah Tannenbaum and Myra Stillman's *Understanding Maps, Charting the Land, Sea, and Sky* (1957). At this time also John Lewellen's *Understanding Electronics* (1957) added much to the older boys' knowledge of intricate modern machines, which do all but human thinking.

Increased interest in the contribution of art to books of scientific fact came into publishing for children with the work of Anthony Ravielli. It seemed as if the care and artistic talent lavished on the picture books of previous decades were now to be given to informative books in science. This was especially evident in *Wonders of the Human Body*, which appeared in 1954 for inter-

mediate and junior high school children. Using a child as an example, Ravielli described the skeleton, the muscles, and the nervous, digestive, and respiratory systems of the human body clearly and imaginatively, demonstrating with his montage technique the informative value of drawings and the quiet beauty which artistic draughtsmanship could lend to factual books. In 1955 the same talent lent distinction to Katherine B. Shippen's story of the growth of scientific theory and experimentation in *Men, Microscopes and Living Things*. By 1957 Ravielli's *An Adventure in Geometry* was hailed as a work of art as well as an imaginatively conceived and significant treatment of a hitherto dull subject.

Similarly, Henry Billings, in his *Bridges,* brought out in 1956, revealed a new trend in informative publications for children. He not only dealt with the evolution of prin-

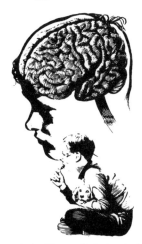

From *Wonders of the Human Body* by Anthony Ravielli. Il. by author. Viking, 1954.

From *An Adventure in Geometry* by Anthony Ravielli. Il. by author. Viking, 1957.

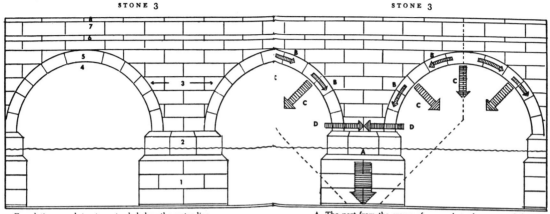

1. Foundation or substructure stands below the water line
2. Piers rest on foundation stones
3. Spandrel or space between arches
4. Crown of the arch or top of the arch
5. Keystone, which holds all the other stones in the arch in place
6. Bottom coping—a projecting line of stones that marks the level of the roadway
7. Parapet or guard rail
8. Top coping that finishes or protects the parapet

A. The part from the crown of one arch to the crown of the next can be considered as one section of the bridge. The total weight of each of the sections is carried by the pier below it.
B. These arrows indicate the locking action, due to compression, of the curved stones that form the arch.
C. These arrows indicate the wedging action not only of the keystone but of all the stones in the arch.
D. There is a sidewise thrust at the point where the arch meets the pier. This is counterbalanced arch by arch until the last arch rests on the abutment.

In relation to the massive dead-weight load carried by each pier, the live load as represented by teams and wagons would be inconsequential. The semicircular stone arch, as used by the

Romans, blocked one-half to two-thirds of the river.

An eighteenth-century bridge like Peronnet's (page 38) took up only one-fifth of the river space.

From *Bridges* by Henry Billings.
Il. by author. Viking, 1956.

ciples of engineering related to bridge building and helped boys and girls to identify different kinds of bridges, but he set the whole project in the social and economic growth of the nation which created

the need for increased access to all parts of the country and an expanded system of transportation. Its drawings and illustrations are not only artistic but are the kind over which boys pore by the hour.

Summary

THE SPURT — NEW PROCESSES AND A DEDICATED LEADERSHIP

Fifty years of children's books—what riches they have brought! Surely no nation on earth has been able to give its children so much in so short a time. While Europe and much of Asia were torn by two great wars, the United States had no fighting on its own soil. Men and women of genius both as artists and authors came from around the world to stimulate and to be stimulated in this country. New processes of printing made possible hitherto unheard of experiments in illustration and typography. Dedicated leadership among our own children's librarians and book designers and editors gave encouragement to talent wherever it was to be found.

CHANGED ATTITUDES TOWARD CHILDREN

Changed attitudes toward children, toward the process of growing up, and toward the purposes of reading made possible new approaches to writing for boys and girls. Children were treated with respect by authors. They were neither to be talked "at" nor "down to." Forces within them were to be stimulated through imaginative presentation of experience and not through preachment and moralizing. Authors began to look at children in their stories as human personalities whether they saw them in their own homes in varying cultures within our national borders, or in other countries of the world—not as pegs on which to hang information or moral discourses. Gay, lively children—and sometimes troubled ones—came alive in the pages of books, not in all books, but in those which stand out through the decades.

BOOKS KEEPING PACE WITH THE CHILDREN'S WORLD

Books have kept pace with the children's world and with the immediacy of the need to know and to understand which confronts every human being today. History in 1910 was mainly the story of battles on land and sea. Today, in distinguished books by distinguished authors, movements and forces are examined in ways which children can understand, illuminating social, economic, and cultural influences in our national life. The place of our nation in the history of the world by periods and in terms of geological and anthropological forces through the centuries has been described in books outstanding in text and illustration.

Picture books for little children have made great events in our country's story come alive for them as in Alice Dalgliesh's *The Thanksgiving Story* (1954); and older children have lived through historic events with characters like those in Walter D. Edmonds's *The Matchlock Gun* (1941), Carol Ryrie Brink's *Caddie Woodlawn* (1935), and Rebecca Caudill's *Tree of Freedom* (1949). Biography, too, has been greatly extended in range of subject, in depth of presentation, and in attractiveness of format. There is still room for more stories of the lives of women for the sake of the girls and more biographies of distinguished people other than the great patriots.

READING RELATED TO VARIOUS MODES OF COMMUNICATION

Television and radio have stimulated reading in an untold number of ways, not only through storytelling and the presentation of literary films and plays, but merely by presenting thrilling discoveries, major events, and new knowledge, all of which make reading about them a necessity. The children's encyclopedias have come into the reading world during these years with their attractive format and their presentation of what children want to know. They are soundly based in scholarship yet written by authorities who know how to appeal to youthful readers.

NEW VALUES IN ANIMAL STORIES

Animal stories abound in colorful picture books for children. There is a wealth of pets with personality like Angus with enticing human qualities which bring little children and animals together. They culminate, however, in sensitive stories like Eric Knight's *Lassie Come-Home* (1940) or Marjorie Kinnan Rawlings's *The Yearling* (1938), in which the life of an animal is intertwined with human values or with natural, social, or historical settings as in Marguerite Henry's *Misty of Chincoteague* (1947).

ACHIEVING A BALANCE BETWEEN FACT AND FANCY

One of the problems persisting throughout the fifty years has been to strike a wise balance in children's reading between fact and imagination and between new and old. The great fairy tales of Europe and of the Middle East have been joined by those of India, of Russia, of South America, of Africa, and of the Orient, as well as by regional and tall tales of our own nation. New editions of them all and of the stories of Greek and Roman and Norse heroes have kept them alive in attractive format. Stories like E. B. White's *Charlotte's Web* (1952) and Mary Norton's *The Borrowers* (1953) have joined Kenneth Grahame's *The Wind in the Willows* (1908) and Charles L. Dodgson's *Alice in Wonderland* (1865) in giving children joy in flights of fancy and release from a too pressing world. Poetry, old and new, has appeared in format unknown fifty years ago and in a range of content to fit every taste. Organized often according to the interests of children, it serves a varied function—sometimes to tell a good story, sometimes to give the charm of novelty to the things of every day, and sometimes to invite escape into the realm of faerie.

THE PERFECTING OF THE PICTURE BOOK

The period from 1925 on will go down in history as the time of the perfecting of the picture book in which text and illustrations in complete harmony carry the narrative together throughout the book. It is the picture story book which maintains the child's interest in reading during the difficult period of learning to read. Throughout the second quarter of the century, the freshness, the originality, the unbelievable variety in theme, in text, and in illustration represented by this new form has revolutionized writing for little children. Titles such as Hardie Gramatky's *Little Toot* (1939), Robert McCloskey's *Make Way for Ducklings* (1941), Edward Ardizzone's *Little Tim and the Brave Sea Captain* (1936), Alvin Tresselt's *White Snow, Bright Snow* (1947), Virginia Lee Burton's *The Little House* (1942), and Wanda Ga'g's *Millions of Cats* (1928) suggest the rich development and artistic contribution of the picture story book to the children's reading world.

KEEPING HUMOR ALIVE

A generous fund of humor, a happy heritage from Randolph Caldecott and others, has taken new and sprightly forms in the last fifty years, whether in the ridiculous nonsense of Dr. Seuss, the hilarious comedy of child life itself as in Robert McCloskey's *Homer Price* (1943) or Keith Robertson's *Henry Reed, Inc.* (1958), in the clever incongruity of Munro Leaf's *The Story of Ferdinand* (1936), in the gentle interpretive quality of Robert Lawson's *Rabbit Hill* (1944) or Carolyn S. Bailey's *Miss Hickory* (1946) or the genial satire of Robert McCloskey's *Lentil* (1940).

CHOOSING BOOKS WISELY

Both research and contact with boys and girls have made teachers and librarians especially conscious of the need for reading materials suited to the wide range of interests and reading ability represented in any normal group of children of the same age. As the school curriculum has broadened, many areas of learning have developed in which new informative materials have had to be prepared. Easy books for beginning readers to read to themselves have appeared to supplement the primary grade reading textbooks. Whole series of informative books in science and history have been projected. Sets of biographies for younger readers and rewritten classics are appearing constantly. Such series—now more than one hundred of them are on the market—are sometimes "boxed" and sold in "sets" regardless of the wide variation in value among the individual books presented. What happens to the library or classroom book fund or to the value and well-rounded character of its book collection under such circumstances depends entirely upon the purchaser's knowledge of other books on the market and on his integrity in refusing "the box" or "the set" and examining each title on its own merits. The need is therefore greater than ever for sending out from teachers colleges and library schools elementary school teachers and librarians well versed in both literary and informative books for children and qualified to judge with care the great array of titles now coming annually from the press.

ACHIEVING COOPERATION AMONG CREATORS, DISPENSERS, AND USERS OF CHILDREN'S BOOKS

The story of the last fifty years is one of remarkable cooperation of authors, artists, publishers, and booksellers, of librarians in school and public libraries, of teachers and supervisors both as individuals and in their national organizations, of scholars in the academic fields, and of directors of teacher education in the field of children's literature. Together they have made notable strides in the improvement and dissemination of books and in the development of a love of reading among boys and girls. The future is in their hands—a future made all the brighter because of the dedication of a distinctive and creative fifty years.

Notes to the Text

[1]Martha Finley (pseudonym Martha Farquharson), *Elsie Dinsmore* (New York: Dodd, 1867). First of a series of twenty-five books ending with *Elsie and Her Namesakes* in 1905. Several titles were published by A. L. Burt in 1930.

[2]Jacob Abbott, The *Rollo* Books. There were sixteen *Rollo* books which appeared between 1834 and 1858. *Rollo Learning to Talk* (1834) was the first, published by John Allen in Boston. The last of this series was *The Rollo Philosophy* (in four parts, published in 1842). Then followed *Rollo's Tour in Europe*, a series of ten volumes from *Rollo on the Atlantic* (Boston: W. J. Reynolds and Company, 1853) to *Rollo in Rome* (Boston: Brown, Taggard, and Chase, 1858).

[3]Rebecca Sophia Clarke (pseud. Sophie May), *Dotty Dimple at Play* (Boston: Lee and Shepard, 1875), pp. 36-49.

[4]Jacob Abbott, *Rollo on the Atlantic, op. cit.*

[5]Alice M. Jordan, *From Rollo to Tom Sawyer and Other Papers* (Boston: The Horn Book, Inc., 1948), p. 76.

[6]Samuel G. Goodrich, *Peter Parley's Book of the United States* (Boston: Charles J. Hendee, 1837), p. 177. Peter Parley was one of the names under which Goodrich and other writers of his day wrote.

[7]Alice M. Jordan, *op. cit.*, p. 21.

[8]Clarence Day, "Noble Boys," *The Saturday Review of Literature*, XV (November 14, 1936), pp. 3-4.

[9]Rebecca Sophia Clarke (pseud. Sophie May), The *Dotty Dimple* Series. The *Dotty Dimple* series ran through seven volumes from 1865 to 1897: *Dotty Dimple* (Boston: Lee and Shepard, 1865); *Dotty Dimple at Home* (1868); *Dotty Dimple at Play* (1875); *Dotty Dimple at Her Grandmother's* (1895); *Dotty Dimple Out West* (1896); *Dotty Dimple at School* (1897); and *Dotty Dimple's Flyaway* (1897).

[10]Sarah Chauncey Woolsey (pseud. Susan Coolidge). There were five books about Katy: *What Katy Did* (Boston: Roberts Brothers, 1873, and Little, 1900, 1911, and 1924); *What Katy Did at School* (Boston: Roberts Brothers, 1874; Little, 1901, 1911, and 1927); *What Katy Did Next* (Boston: Roberts Brothers, 1886; Little, 1901, 1911, and 1930); *Clover* (Boston: Roberts Brothers, 1888; Little, 1901 and 1913); and *In the High Valley* (Boston: Roberts Brothers, 1891; Little, 1901 and 1913).

[11]Harriet M. Lothrop (pseud. Margaret Sidney). *Five Little Peppers and How They Grew* (Boston: D. Lothrop and Company, 1880) was the first of a long series of *Five Little Peppers* books, including *Five Little Peppers Midway* (1890); *Five Little Peppers Grown Up* (1892); *Phronsie Pepper, the Last of the Five Little Peppers* (1897); and others. Later editions of many of them followed from 1900 on, with a final edition published by Houghton in 1937. A new edition of *Five Little Peppers* was put out by the World Publishing Company in Cleveland and New York in 1950. Another came from the Macmillan Company in 1962.

[12]Annie Fellows Johnston, *The Little Colonel* (Boston: Joseph Knight Company, 1896). The series ran to 1907, published by L. C. Page of Boston (*The Little Colonel's Knight Comes Riding*, 1907). Reissues by Farrar persisted until 1929. In 1959 Random House (New York) published *The Little Colonel* with Laura E. H. Richards's *Captain January*.

[13]Mrs. Laura E. H. Richards, *Queen Hildegarde* (Boston: Estes and Lauriat, 1889). Other titles in the series came out until 1897: *Hildegarde's Holiday* (1891); *Hildegarde's Home* (1892); *Hildegarde's Neighbors* (1895); and *Hildegarde's Harvest* (1897).

[14]Mrs. Laura E. H. Richards, *The Three Margarets* (Boston: Estes and Lauriat, 1897). This, the first of the *Three Margarets* series, was followed by *Margaret Montfort* (1898); *Peggy* (1899); and *Rita* (1900).

[15]W. W. Charters, "Adolescent Boys' Preferences, 1907-1917," *School and Society*, XI (March 13, 1920), pp. 323-324.

[16]Samuel McChord Crothers, *Miss Muffet's Christmas Party* (Boston: Houghton Mifflin, 1902), pp. 14-15.

[17]F. J. Harvey Darton, *Children's Books in England* (Cambridge: Cambridge University Press, 1958), p. 236.

[18]Caroline Marie Hewins, "Work with Children in Connecticut," *Library Work with Children,* edited by Alice I. Hazeltine (New York: H. W. Wilson Company, 1917), p. 48.

[19]Frank Gruber, *Horatio Alger, Jr., A Biography and Bibliography of the Best-Selling Author of All Time* (West Los Angeles: Grover Jones Press, 1961).

[20]Alice M. Jordan, *From Rollo to Tom Sawyer and Other Papers, op. cit.,* pp. 30-31.

[21]Charles Austin Fosdick (pseud. Harry Castlemon). See Jacob Blanck's bibliography, *Harry Castlemon, Boys' Own Author* (New York: R. R. Bowker, 1941).

[22]Edward Stratemeyer was the founder of the Stratemeyer Syndicate which published many of the juvenile series with boy and girl characters who did surpassing things. He wrote under many pseudonyms, some of which follow.

[23]Arthur Winfield, pseud., writer of the *Rover Boys* series, 1899-1925; (New York: Mershon, 1899): *The Rover Boys at School; The Rover Boys on the Ocean; The Rover Boys in the Jungle;* through eighteen more volumes to *The Rover Boys on the Sunset Trail,* published by Grosset & Dunlap in New York in 1925.

[24]Clarence Young, pseud., was writer of the *Motor Boys* series, fifteen titles of which were published by Cupples in New York between *The Motor Boys* in 1906 and *The Motor Boys on Thunder Mountain* in 1924.

[25]Victor Appleton, pseud., writer of the *Tom Swift* series, published by Grosset & Dunlap in New York from 1910 to the present. Typical are the following from the earlier and later (*Tom Swift Junior*) series: *Tom Swift and His Motor Cycle* (1910); *Tom Swift and His Electric Runabout* (1910); *Tom Swift and His Airship* (1910); *Tom Swift and His Submarine* (1910); *Tom Swift and the Caves of Nuclear Fire* (1956); *Tom Swift and His Ultrasonic Cycloplane* (1957); and *Tom Swift and a Visitor from Planet X* (1961).

[26]Laura Lee Hope, pseud., author of the *Bobbsey Twins* series. The first volume, *The Bobbsey Twins,* was published by Mershon in New York in 1904; *The Bobbsey Twins at London Tower,* the fifty-fifth volume in the series, was published by Grosset & Dunlap (New York) in 1959. The series is still being added to yearly.

[27]Russell B. Nye, "Fifty Years with Tom Swift," *The Progressive,* 24 (December, 1960), pp. 37-40.

[28]Franklin K. Mathiews, "Making Worth While Boys' Recreational Reading," *Public Libraries,* 21 (July, 1916), p. 302.

[29]*Ibid.,* p. 301.

[30]Frederic G. Melcher, "Thirty Years of Children's Books," *The Children's Library Yearbook,* No. 1 (Chicago: American Library Association, 1929), p 7.

[31]Horace E. Scudder's *Bodley* family appeared in eight volumes between 1875 and 1890. *Doings of the Bodley Family* (New York: Hurd, 1875); *The Bodleys on Wheels* (Boston: Houghton, 1879); *The Bodleys Afloat* (Boston: Houghton, 1880: new edition, 1907); and *The Bodley Grandchildren and Their Journey in Holland* (Boston: Houghton, 1882) are typical.

[32]Hezekiah Butterworth. The *Zigzag Journeys* series (Boston: Estes and Lauriat) of seventeen volumes opened with *Zigzag Journeys in Europe* (1880) and closed with *Zigzag Journeys around the World* (1895).

[33]The *Little Journeys* series was published by Flanagan in Chicago (thirty-six volumes in all) between 1900 and 1911. The first was Marion M. George's *A Little Journey to Cuba* (1900), and the last was George W. James's *A Little Journey to Some Strange Places and People in Our Southwestern Land* (1911), with new editions or reprints up to 1931.

[34]The *Boy Travellers* series (New York: Harper, 1880-1928) in fifteen volumes with T. W. Knox as editor appeared between 1880 and 1908 with new editions up to 1928. The first was *Boy Travellers in the Far East,* and the last was *Boy Travellers in the Far East, Part II.*

[35]The *Little People Everywhere* series (Boston: Little, 1909-1916) contained fifteen volumes written by Mrs. Etta A. McDonald and Julia Dalrymple. The first was *Rafael in Italy* (1909), and the last, *Chandra in India* (1916).

[36]Macmillan's *Peeps at Many Lands* series (New York: 1907-1933) contained relatively mature texts and many beautiful colored illustrations. The initial four volumes published in 1907 were Mrs. Beatrix Jungman's *Peeps at Holland* and J. Finnemore's

Peeps at India, *Peeps at Italy*, and *Peeps at Japan*. The last volume, published in 1935, was E. Fulan's *Peeps at Morocco*.

[37]The *Our Little Cousins* series (Boston: Page, 1901-1909) contained forty-two titles, nineteen of them by Mary H. Wade. *Our Little Brown Cousin* by Mary Wade appeared in 1901, and *Our Little Persian Cousin* by Ephraim C. Shedd, in 1909. Reprints appeared up to 1930.

[38]Corinne Bacon (ed.), *Children's Catalog of 2000 Books* (New York and White Plains: H. W. Wilson Company, 1916), p. 170.

[39]Mary Mapes Dodge, "The Hero of Harlem," *Hans Brinker or The Silver Skates* (New York: Charles Scribner's Sons, 1958), pp. 136-140.

[40]Jane Andrews, *The Seven Little Sisters Who Live on the Round Ball That Floats in the Air* (Boston: Tichnor and Fields, 1861), p. 6.

[41]Robert Spiller, *et al.*, *Literary History of the United States* (New York: The Macmillan Company, 1955), p. 974.

[42]W. W. Charters, "Adolescent Boys' Preferences, 1907-1917," *School and Society*, XI (March 13, 1920), pp. 323-324.

Irving Harlow Hart, "Best Sellers in Fiction during the First Quarter of the Twentieth Century," *Publishers' Weekly*, 107 (February 14, 1925), pp. 525-527.

[43]Irvin Cobb, *Irvin Cobb at His Best* (Garden City: The Sun Dial Press, 1940), p. 170.

[44]Jane Andrews, *The Stories Mother Nature Told Her Children* (Boston: Ginn and Company, 1889), pp. vii-viii.

[45]Thornton W. Burgess, *Old Mother West Wind*, Golden Anniversary Edition (Boston: Little, Brown and Company, 1960), pp. 3-6. (First Edition, 1910.)

[46]Carlo Lorenzini (pseud. C. Collodi), *The Adventures of Pinocchio*, was first printed in Florence, Italy, in 1882. It appeared in English translation (translated by M. A. Murray) in London in 1892, published by Unwin. An American edition with an introduction by Hezekiah Butterworth was published in Boston by Jordan, Marsh and Company in 1898.

[47]From time to time, publishers have brought out for new generations of children new editions of some of the old classics. Among them are such as these, recommended in the *Children's Catalog*: Lamb's *Tales* (New York: Macmillan, 1923); *Rip Van Winkle and the Legend of Sleepy Hollow*, il. by Maud and Miska Petersham (New York: Macmillan, 1951); *Alice's Adventures in Wonderland, and Through the Looking Glass*, il. by John Tenniel (New York: Macmillan, 1932); *At the Back of the North Wind* (New York: Macmillan, 1924); *Uncle Remus: His Songs and Sayings*, Revised Edition, il. by A. B. Frost (New York: Appleton, 1947); *The Adventures of Pinocchio*, il. by Attilio Mussino (New York: Macmillan, 1925); *The Jungle Book, The Second Jungle Book, The Just So Stories* (all New York: Doubleday, 1946); *The Fables of Aesop* (New York: Macmillan, 1950). *Arabian Nights*, il. by Vera Bock (New York: Longmans, 1946), is recommended in the ALA's *A Basic Book Collection for Elementary Grades*, 1960.

[48]Frances Clarke Sayers, "Preface," *The Wind in the Willows*, by Kenneth Grahame (New York: Charles Scribner's Sons, 1960), p. v.

[49]Ernest H. Shepard, "Illustrating *The Wind in the Willows*," *The Horn Book Magazine*, XXX (April, 1954), p. 84.

[50]F. J. Harvey Darton, *Children's Books in England* (Cambridge: Cambridge University Press, 1958), p. 219. Arguments are still going on concerning the exact date. Darton refers to editions of 1719, 1729, and 1741 (p. 87). In the catalog of the exhibit of *Children's Literature, Books and Manuscripts* at the Pierpont Morgan Library in New York from November, 1954, through February, 1955, there appeared what was listed as "the first edition of Perrault in English," entitled *Histories or Tales of Past Times*. It was published in English in 1729, dedicated to the Countess of Granville by Robert Samber, and contained such tales as "The Little Red Riding Hood," "The Blue Beard," "The Sleeping Beauty," "The Master Cat or Puss in Boots," and "Cinderella or The Glass Slipper." The catalog was published by the library in 1954.

[51]Four editions of Andersen's stories were made available in English in 1846: Mrs. Howitt's; a translation by Charles Boner called *A Danish Story Book*, published by Joseph Cundall in London; another by the same translator and publisher called *The Nightingale and Three Other Stories*; and

Danish Fairy Legends and Tales, translated by Caroline Peachey and published by William Pickering in London.

[52]F. J. Harvey Darton, *op. cit.,* p. 248.

[53]Andrew Lang's *Blue Fairy Book* appeared in 1889, published by Longmans in New York and London. The *Lilac Fairy Book,* the last of the series, came out of Longmans in New York in 1910. The more popular tales went through several editions, the last in 1947 and 1948.

[54]Paul Hazard, *Books, Children and Men* (Boston: The Horn Book, Inc., 1944), pp. 80-85.

[55]Cornelia Meigs, *et al., A Critical History of Children's Literature* (New York: The Macmillan Company, 1953), pp. 248-249.

[56]Walter Crane (il.), *The Baby's Opera* (London: Routledge, 1876); *The Baby's Bouquet* (London: Warne, 1878); and *Goody Two Shoes Picture Book, 1 and 2* (London: John Lane, 1901).

[57]Bertha E. Mahony, Louise Payson Latimer, and Beulah Folmsbee, *Illustrators of Children's Books, 1744-1945* (Boston: The Horn Book, Inc., 1947), p. 71.

[58]Howard Pyle, *Pepper and Salt* (New York: Harper, 1885), p. viii.

[59]Kate Greenaway, *A Apple Pie* (London: Routledge, 1886).

[60]Anne Carroll Moore, "From the Children's Holiday Books of 1918," *The Bookman,* XLVIII (November, 1918), p. 470.

[61]Clement Moore's "A Visit from St. Nicholas" was first published anonymously in the *Troy Sentinel,* a newspaper in Troy, New York, in 1823. It appeared in book form on page 28 of *The New-York Book of Poetry* edited by Charles F. Hoffman and published by G. Dearborn of New York in 1837.

[62]A possible exception is Roger Ingpen's *One Thousand Poems for Children* (Philadelphia: Jacobs, 1903). It was so completely revised by Elizabeth Sechrist (Philadelphia: Macrae Smith, 1946) that in both choice of selections and in arrangement it seems a different book.

[63]William E. Henley, *Lyra Heroica* (New York: Charles Scribner's Sons, 1891), pp. vii-viii.

[64]Edward V. Lucas, *A Book of Verses for Children* (London: G. Richards, 1897), p. iii.

[65]Louey Chisholm, *The Golden Staircase* (New York: G. P. Putnam's Sons, 1907), p. vi.

[66]Kate Douglas Wiggin and Nora Archibald Smith, *Golden Numbers* (Garden City: Doubleday, Doran and Company, 1903 and 1923), pp. xl-xli.

[67]Walter de la Mare, *A Child's Day* (New York: E. P. Dutton and Company, 1915), pp. 6-7.

[68]*Ibid.,* p. 6.

[69]Paul Hazard, *Books, Children and Men, op. cit.,* pp. 42-43.

[70]Louis Untermeyer, *This Singing World; An Anthology of Modern Poetry for Young People* (New York: Harcourt, Brace and Company, 1923), p. 1.

[71]Elmer Boyd Smith, *The Farm Book* (1910); *The Seashore Book* (1912); and *The Railroad Book* (1913); all published by the Houghton Mifflin Company in Boston and New York.

[72]Hendrik W. Van Loon, *The Story of Mankind* (New York: Liveright Publishing Corporation, 1921, rev. 1951), p. x (1951).

[73]*Ibid.,* p. 465 (1951).

[74]Virgil M. Hillyer, *A Child's History of the World* (New York: Appleton-Century-Crofts, 1924 and 1951), p. xi (1951).

[75]*Ibid.,* p. ix (1951).

[76]Bertha M. Mahony and Elinor Whitney, *Realms of Gold in Children's Books* (New York: Doubleday, Doran and Company, 1929), p. 552.

[77]Frederic G. Melcher, "Thirty Years of Children's Books," *The Children's Library Yearbook,* No. 1 (Chicago: American Library Association, 1929), p. 6.

[78]Caroline M. Hewins, *Books for Boys and Girls* (Chicago: American Library Association, 1915), p. 6.

[79]"Books for the Young," *The Atlantic Monthly,* LXX (December, 1892), p. 853.

[80]Alice M. Jordan, *From Rollo to Tom Sawyer and Other Papers, op. cit.,* pp. 113-117.

[81]Anne Carroll Moore, *My Roads to Childhood* (Boston: The Horn Book, Inc., 1961). See also three volumes of *The Three Owls,* published by Coward-McCann in 1925, 1928, and 1931.

[82]James Daugherty, "Illustrating for Children," *Reading without Boundaries* (New York: New York Public Library, 1956), p. 570.

[83]Frances Clarke Sayers, "Big Walking Day," *Reading without Boundaries, op. cit.,* p. 563.

[84]James Daugherty, *Reading without Boundaries,* op. cit., p. 570.

[85]Harriet G. Long, *Rich the Treasure* (Chicago: American Library Association, 1953), p. 56.

[86]*Statistics of Public Libraries: 1955-56* (Biennial Survey of Education in the United States—1954-56, Chapter 5) (Washington: U. S. Department of Health, Education, and Welfare, Government Printing Office), p. 25.

[87]"San Francisco Proceedings of the American Association of School Librarians," *American Library Association Bulletin,* 41 (September 15, 1947), pp. 39-40.

[88]Franklin T. Baker, *A Bibliography of Children's Reading* (New York: Teachers College, Columbia University, 1908), p. 1.

[89]*Ibid.,* p. 4.

[90]*Ibid.,* p. 7.

[91]*Ibid.,* pp. 6-7.

[92]James F. Hosic, "The Conduct of a Course in Children's Literature," *Journal of Proceedings and Addresses* (Washington: National Education Association, July, 1913), pp. 730-40.

[93]National Council of Teachers of English, *The National Interest and the Teaching of English* (Champaign, Ill.: The Council, 1961), p. 58.

[94]Alfred H. Grommon (ed.), *The Education of Teachers of English for American Schools and Colleges* (New York: Appleton-Century-Crofts, 1963), Chapter 2.

[95]United States Department of Health, Education, and Welfare, *Public School Library Statistics, 1958-59* (Washington: The Department, October, 1960), p. 1.

[96]James F. Hosic, Chairman, National Joint Committee on English Representing the Commission on the Reorganization of Secondary Education of the National Education Association and the National Council of Teachers of English, *The Reorganization of English in Secondary Schools,* Bulletin, 1917, No. 2, United States Bureau of Education (Washington: Government Printing Office, 1917), p. 45.

[97]"Books of the Year for Children," *Child Study,* 37:1 (Winter, 1959-60), pp. 29-32. Available separately from the Child Study Association of America, 19 East 89th Street, New York 28, New York.

[98]The Children's Book Council, 175 Fifth Avenue, New York 10, New York.

[99]Bertha Mahony Miller and Elinor Whitney Field, *Newbery Medal Books: 1922-1955; Horn Book Papers,* Volume I (Boston: The Horn Book, Inc., 1955), p. 4.

[100]*The Horn Book Magazine,* I:1 (October, 1924), p. 30.

[101]*The Horn Book Magazine,* The Horn Book, Inc. (Boston: 585 Boylston Street).

[102]*Elementary English,* An official organ of the National Council of Teachers of English, 508 South Sixth Street, Champaign, Illinois. John J. De Boer of the University of Illinois served as the distinguished editor of *Elementary English* from 1942 to May, 1961. Its present editor is William A. Jenkins of the University of Wisconsin—Milwaukee.

[103]C. C. Certain, "Dr. Dolittle, the Children and the Droll 'Huge' Lofting," *The Elementary English Review,* I (May, 1924), pp. 90-92.

[104]Helen K. Mackintosh, "A Study of Children's Choices in Poetry," *The Elementary English Review,* I (May, 1924), pp. 85-89.

[105]Wilma L. Garnett, "A Study of Children's Choices in Prose," *The Elementary English Review,* I (June, 1924), pp. 133-137.

[106]Martha Caroline Pritchard, "The Beginnings of an Elementary School Library," *The Elementary English Review,* I (May, 1924), p. 111.

[107]C. C. Certain, "An Elementary School Library in Dollars and Cents," *The Elementary English Review,* II (March, 1925), pp. 101-105.

[108]Carleton W. Washburne, *Adjusting the School to the Child* (Yonkers: The World Book Company, 1932).

Evelyn Dewey, *The Dalton Laboratory Plan* (New York: E. P. Dutton and Company, 1922).

[109]Robert H. Beck, Walter W. Cook, and Nolan K. Kearney, *Curriculum in the Modern Elementary School,* Second Edition (Englewood Cliffs, N. J.: Prentice-Hall, 1960), p. 49.

[110]Anne Carroll Moore, "Children under Ten and Their Books," *The Bookman,* L (1919-20), pp. 640-642.

[111]Lucy Sprague Mitchell, *Here and Now Story Book, Two- to Seven-Year-Olds* (New York: E. P. Dutton, 1921).

[112]*Ibid.,* p. 3.

[113]Lucy Sprague Mitchell, *Another Here and Now Story Book, Two- to Seven-Year-Olds* (New York: E. P. Dutton, 1937).

[114]Lucy Sprague Mitchell, *Here and Now Story Book,* New Edition, revised and enlarged (New York: E. P. Dutton, 1948).

[115]*Ibid.,* p. 16 (1948).

[116]H. E. Wheeler, "The Psychological Case Against the Fairy Tale," *The Elementary School Journal,* XXIX (June, 1929), pp. 754-755.

[117]Hamilton Wright Mabie, *Fairy Tales Every Child Should Know* (New York: Doubleday and Company, 1914), pp. vi-vii.

[118]Elizabeth Enright, "The Hero's Changing Face," *The Contents of the Basket* (New York: New York Public Library, 1960), p. 28.

[119]Florence V. Barry, *A Century of Children's Books* (New York: The Doran Company, 1923), p. 193. For another statement of both sides of this controversy see Frances Clarke Sayers and Dora V. Smith, "Lose Not the Nightingale," *American Library Association Bulletin,* 31 (October 1, 1937), pp. 621-628, and 32 (January, 1938), pp. 7-13.

[120]May Massee, "Children's Books on Demand," *Reading without Boundaries, op. cit.,* p. 582.

[121]For acceptance papers and discussions about the winners and their works, see Bertha Mahony Miller and Elinor Whitney Field, *Caldecott Medal Books: 1938-57, Horn Book Papers,* Volume II (Boston: The Horn Book, Inc., 1957), and Irene Smith Green, *History of the Newbery and Caldecott Awards* (New York: The Viking Press, 1957).

[122]May Lamberton Becker, *First Adventures in Reading* (New York: Frederick A. Stokes and Company, 1936), pp. 14-19.

[123]Bertha Mahony Miller and Elinor Whitney Field, *Newbery Medal Books: 1922-1955* (Boston: The Horn Book, Inc., 1955), p. 99.

[124]Robert Lawson, "Make Me a Child Again," *The Horn Book Magazine,* XVI (November-December, 1940), p. 450, or Phyllis Fenner, *Something Shared: Children and Books* (New York: The John Day Company, 1959), pp. 47-48.

[125]Henry Cavendish, "Come Visit Poet Frost for a New Look at Life," *The Miami News* (February 15, 1959), Section B, p. 5.

[126]"The Laura Ingalls Wilder Award," *The Horn Book Magazine,* XXX (August, 1954), p. 243.

[127]Virgil M. Hillyer, *A Child's Geography of the World* (New York: Appleton-Century-Crofts, 1929 and 1951), p. xvii (1951).

[128]Virgil M. Hillyer, *A Child's History of Art* (New York: Appleton-Century-Crofts, 1933, rev. 1951).

[129]James Daugherty, *Daniel Boone* (New York: The Viking Press, 1939), p. 5.

[130]*To Enrich Young Life* (Garden City, N. Y.: Junior Literary Guild, 1939).

[131]Nora Beust, *500 Books for Children,* Bulletin, 1939, No. 11, United States Office of Education (Washington: Superintendent of Documents, 1940).

[132]Association for Childhood Education International, *A Bibliography of Books for Young Children* (1937, 1942, 1946); after and including 1948, *Bibliography of Books for Children* revised biennially to date. *Children's Books for $1.25 or Less,* prepared by Elizabeth H. Gross, is illustrative of their pamphlet on less expensive books for children. (Washington: The Association, 3615 Wisconsin Avenue, N. W.).

[133]Association for Childhood Education International, *Childhood Education,* 3615 Wisconsin Avenue, N.W., Washington 16, D. C.

[134]Eloise Ramsey, Chairman, Committee on a Recreational Reading List for Elementary Schools of the National Council of Teachers of English, *Reading for Fun* (Chicago: The Council, 1937).

[135]National Council of Teachers of English, *Adventuring with Books,* for $.75. (Champaign, Ill.: The Council, 508 South Sixth Street).

[136]National Education Association and the American Library Association, *Schools and Public Libraries Working Together in School Library Service* (Washington: National Education Association, 1941).

[137]Phyllis Fenner, *Our Library* (New York: The John Day Company, 1942). Also *The Proof of the Pudding* (New York: The John Day Company, 1957).

[138]Ellen Lewis Buell, "Big Spring Lists Offer Variety in Children's Books," *Publishers' Weekly,* 142 (April 18, 1942), p. 1481.

[139]Frederic G. Melcher, Editorial, *Publishers' Weekly,* 142 (April 18, 1942), p. 1443.

[140]Agnes De Lima, "Children's Reading in Wartime," *Publishers' Weekly,* 142 (April 18, 1942), p. 1485.

[141]*Ibid.,* pp. 1483-1484.

[142]*Ibid.,* p. 1486.

[143]Child Study Association of America, Inc., *Read-to-Me Storybook* (1947); *Read Me Another Story* (1949); *Read Me More Stories* (1951); *Read to Yourself Storybook* (1953); *More Read to Yourself Stories: Fun and Magic* (1956). All have been published by Thomas Y. Crowell Company.

[144]Margaret Lesser, "The Impossible Is Happening," *Publishers' Weekly,* 144 (August 28, 1943), pp. 686-687.

[145]"International Youth Book Exhibit at Munich," *Publishers' Weekly,* 150 (August 31, 1946), pp. 997-998.

[146]Rebecca Caudill, *Tree of Freedom* (New York: The Viking Press, 1949), p. 263.

[147]Editorial, *Publishers' Weekly,* 144 (August 28, 1943), p. 673.

[148]American Institute of Graphic Arts, *Instructions to Exhibitors for 1937-40 Exhibition of Children's Books* (New York: The Institute, 1940).

[149]The brochures may be purchased from the American Institute of Graphic Arts, 50 East 40th Street, New York 15, New York.

[150]Mary H. Mahar, "The National Defense Education Act, School Librarians, and School Libraries," *Wilson Library Bulletin,* 33 (June, 1959), pp. 737-738. See also the American Association for the Advancement of Science, *The Science Book List,* prepared under the direction of Hilary J. Deason for the Association and the National Science Foundation (Washington: The Association, 1959).

[151]Louise Bonino, "The Landmark Story," *Publishers' Weekly,* 170 (July 30, 1956), pp. 460-463.

[152]"Juvenile Forecast—Series," *Publishers' Weekly,* 182 (July 2, 1962), pp. 199-206.

[153]Helen Sill, "Please, Sir, I Want Some More," *Wilson Library Bulletin,* 29 (November, 1954), pp. 236-239.

[154]Mary Elizabeth Edes, "Some Very Crowded Bandwagons," *Publishers' Weekly,* 178 (July 4, 1960), p. 169.

[155]Martha O. Condit, "Trade Books for Beginning Readers," *Wilson Library Bulletin,* 34 (December, 1959), pp. 284-301. For the complete research study, address Dr. Mary Gaver, Graduate Library School, Rutgers University.

Elizabeth Guilfoile, *Books for Beginning Readers* (Champaign, Ill.: National Council of Teachers of English, 1962).

Frieda M. Heller, "I Can Read It Myself," Bulletin No. 1, Study of Independent Reading, Center for School Experimentation (Columbus: College of Education, Ohio State University, 1960).

David H. Russell, "An Evaluation of Some Easy-to-Read Trade Books for Children," *Elementary English,* XXXVIII (November, 1961), pp. 475-482.

[156]*Library Journal* and *School Library Journal,* R. R. Bowker Company, 1180 Avenue of the Americas, New York, New York.

[157]Miriam B. Snow (compiler), *A Basic Book Collection for Elementary Grades,* Seventh Edition (Chicago: American Library Association, 1960). Also *Notable Children's Books of the Year,* Children's Services Division, American Library Association, 50 East Huron Street, Chicago 11, Illinois; appears as an article in the April issue of the *American Library Association Bulletin.*

[158]Elementary School Book List Committee, *Adventuring with Books* (Champaign, Ill.: National Council of Teachers of English, 1960).

[159]*Bulletin of the Center for Children's Books,* 5835 Kimbark Avenue, Chicago, Illinois.

[160]Mary Peacock Douglas, *Teacher-Librarian's Handbook,* Second Edition (Chicago: American Library Association, 1949). Also *The Pupil Assistant in the School Library* (Chicago: American Library Association, 1957).

[161]Frances Henne and Ruth Ersted, Co-chairmen, Committee on School Library Standards of the American Association of School Librarians, *Standards for School Library Programs* (Chicago: American Library Association, 1960).

[162]*Weekly Reader* Children's Book Club, Education Center, Columbus 16, Ohio.

[163]*Parents' Magazine*'s Book Club for Children, The Parents' Institute, Inc., 52 Vanderbilt Avenue, New York 17, New York.

[164]The Catholic Children's Book Club, 262 East Fourth Street, St. Paul 1, Minnesota.

[165]The Book-of-the-Month Club, Inc., Young Readers of America Book Club, 345 Hudson Street, New York 14, New York.

[166]The Arrow Book Club, Scholastic Book Services, 904 Sylvan Avenue, Englewood Cliffs, New Jersey.

[167]Cornelia Meigs, *et al., A Critical History of Children's Literature* (New York: The Macmillan Company, 1953), p. 590.

[168]Samuel McChord Crothers, "The Enjoyment of Poetry," *The Gentle Reader* (Boston: Houghton Mifflin, 1903), p. 35.

[169]Elizabeth Yates, *Amos Fortune, Free Man* (New York: E. P. Dutton and Company, 1950), p. 26.

[170]Harold Coy, *The Americans* (Boston: Little, Brown and Company, 1958), p. v.

[171]Lynd Ward, "The Book Artist: Ideas and Techniques," pp. 14-35 in *Illustrators of Children's Books, 1946-56*, edited by Ruth Hill Viguers, Marcia Dalphin, and Bertha Mahony Miller (Boston: The Horn Book, Inc., 1958), p. 23.

Significant Books of 1910-1959

Date	Author	Title	Publishers	Grades	Page
THE REALM OF THE IMAGINATION					
1908	Grahame, Kenneth	*The Wind in the Willows* (also: il. by Ernest H. Shepard, 1933 and 1960)	Scribner	4-6	12, 67, 92
1911	Barrie, Sir James M.	*Peter and Wendy* (rev. ed. *Peter Pan*, il. by Nora S. Unwin, 1950)	Scribner	4-6	17
1918	Hudson, William H.	*A Little Boy Lost*	Knopf	6-8	17
1922	Lofting, Hugh	*The Voyages of Dr. Dolittle*	Stokes (Lippincott)	4-7	17
1922	Sandburg, Carl	*Rootabaga Stories* (reprinted with *Rootabaga Pigeons*, n.d.)	Harcourt	5-7	17
1928	Ga'g, Wanda	*Millions of Cats*	Coward	K-3	34, 92
1929	Field, Rachel	*Hitty, Her First Hundred Years*	Macmillan	5-8	38
1934	Travers, Pamela L.	*Mary Poppins*	Harcourt	4-7	39
1939	Bunyan, John	*Pilgrim's Progress* retold by Mary Godolphin	Lippincott	6-8	39
1943	Thurber, James	*Many Moons*	Harcourt	4-5	57
1946	Bailey, Caroline S.	*Miss Hickory*	Viking	4-6	57
1948	Gannett, Ruth S.	*My Father's Dragon*	Random	2-4	58, 67
1952	White, E. B.	*Charlotte's Web*	Harper	4-6	74, 92
1953	Norton, Mary	*The Borrowers*	Harcourt	4-7	75, 92
HEROES OLD AND NEW					
1918	Colum, Padraic	*The Adventures of Odysseus and the Tale of Troy*	Macmillan	6-9	16
1921	Colum, Padraic	*The Golden Fleece and the Heroes Who Lived before Achilles*	Macmillan	7-9	17
1937	Bowman, James C.	*Pecos Bill, the Greatest Cowboy of All Time*	Whitman	6-9	39
1937	Seredy, Kate	*The White Stag*	Viking	6-9	33
1946	Pyle, Howard	*The Merry Adventures of Robin Hood of Great Renown in Nottinghamshire* (first pub. 1883, new ed. 1946)	Scribner	5-9	9
1947	Hosford, Dorothy	*By His Own Might*	Holt	6-8	58
1949	Rounds, Glen	*Ol' Paul, the Mighty Logger* (first pub. 1936)	Holiday	4-9	58
1950	Brown, Marcia	*Dick Whittington and His Cat* (told and cut in linoleum by Marcia Brown)	Scribner	K-3	77
1951	Homer	The *Iliad of Homer* retold by A. J. Church (first pub. 1907 as *The Iliad for Boys and Girls*)	Macmillan	6-9	13

Date	Author	Title	Publishers	Grades	Page
1951	Homer	The *Odyssey of Homer* retold by A. J. Church (first pub. 1906 as *The Odyssey for Boys and Girls*)	Macmillan	6-9	13
1958	Busoni, Rafaello	*The Man Who Was Don Quixote*	Prentice-Hall	7-9	83

FAIRY AND FOLK TALES AND FABLES

Date	Author	Title	Publishers	Grades	Page
1924	Finger, Charles J.	*Tales from Silver Lands*	Doubleday	5-7	17
1928	D'Aulnoy, Mme. La Comtesse	*The White Cat and Other Old French Fairy Tales*	Macmillan (o.p.)	5-7	38
1930	Coatsworth, Elizabeth	*The Cat Who Went to Heaven* (new ed. 1958)	Macmillan	4-7	34
1938	Andersen, Hans C.	*It's Perfectly True and Other Stories* (tr. by Paul Leyssac)	Harcourt	5-8	39
1938	Bishop, Claire H.	*The Five Chinese Brothers*	Coward	1-3	35
1943	Chase, Richard	*Jack Tales*	Houghton	4-6	51
1949	Andersen, Hans C.	*The Emperor's New Clothes* (il. by Virginia Lee Burton)	Houghton	2-5	58
1950	Rackham, Arthur	*Arthur Rackham Fairy Book* (first pub. 1933, new ed. with new illustrations 1950)	Lippincott	4-6	75
1953	Sawyer, Ruth	*Journey Cake, Ho!*	Viking	K-3	76
1957	Asbjörnsen, Peter C., and Moe, Jörgen E.	*The Three Billy Goats Gruff* (il. by Marcia Brown)	Harcourt	K-2	77
1958	Cooney, Barbara	*Chanticleer and the Fox* (adap. from Chaucer and il.)	Crowell	K-3	77
1959	Perrault, Charles	*Puss in Boots* (il. by Hans Fischer)	Harcourt	K-3	78

POETRY

Date	Author	Title	Publishers	Grades	Page
1913	De la Mare, Walter	*Peacock Pie* (new ed. il. by Barbara Cooney, Knopf, 1961)	Holt (o.p.)	4-8	18
1916	Wright, Blanche F. (il.)	*The Real Mother Goose* (new ed. 1960)	Rand	K-3	18
1920	Fyleman, Rose	*Fairies and Chimneys*	Doubleday	3-6	19
1923	Brooke, Leslie (ed.)	*Ring o' Roses*	Warne	K-3	17
1923	De la Mare, Walter (comp.)	*Come Hither* (reset and reprinted from new plates, il. by Warren Chappell, Knopf, 1957)	Knopf (o.p.)	6-10	19
1923	Untermeyer, Louis (ed. and collector)	*This Singing World; An Anthology of Modern Poetry for Young People*	Harcourt	5-9	19, 44
1924	Milne, A. A.	*When We Were Very Young* (il. by Ernest H. Shepard) (in "The Pooh Library," 1961)	Dutton	1-4	19, 43, 79
1926	Field, Rachel	*Taxis and Toadstools*	Doubleday	3-5	43
1928	Lindsay, Vachel	*Johnny Appleseed and Other Poems*	Macmillan	5-9	43
1930	Harrington, Mildred P. (comp.)	*Ring-A-Round*	Macmillan	K-3	43
1930	Teasdale, Sara	*Stars To-Night*	Macmillan	5-8	43
1935	Untermeyer, Louis (ed.)	*Rainbow in the Sky*	Harcourt	K-6	44

Date	Author	Title	Publishers	Grades	Page
1937	Brewton, John E. (comp.)	*Under the Tent of the Sky*	Macmillan	K-5	44
1945	Petersham, Maud and Miska	*The Rooster Crows*	Macmillan	K-3	59
1948	Adshead, Gladys L., and Duff, Annis (comps.)	*An Inheritance of Poetry*	Houghton	K-9	59
1949	Behn, Harry	*The Little Hill*	Harcourt	2-4	78
1954	De Angeli, Marguerite (il. and collector)	*Book of Nursery and Mother Goose Rhymes*	Doubleday	K-3	78
1955	Langstaff, John	*Frog Went A-Courtin'*	Harcourt	K-3	76
1955	Plotz, Helen (comp.)	*Imagination's Other Place*	Crowell	7-9	79
1956	Read, Herbert (ed.)	*This Way, Delight*	Pantheon	4-10	79
1957	Ferris, Helen (ed.)	*Favorite Poems, Old and New*	Doubleday	3-8	79
1959	Frost, Robert	*You Come Too; Favorite Poems of Robert Frost for Young Readers*	Holt	7-9	79

BOYS AND GIRLS—THEIR DOINGS AND ESCAPADES

Date	Author	Title	Publishers	Grades	Page
1917	Canfield, Dorothy	*Understood Betsy*	Holt	5-8	20
1924	Clark, Margery	*The Poppy Seed Cakes*	Doubleday	2-4	18, 33
1926	Milne, A. A.	*Winnie-the-Pooh* (new ed., 1954) (in "The Pooh Library," 1961)	Dutton	3-5	38
1927	Nicholson, William	*Clever Bill* (new ed. 1961)	Doubleday (o.p.)	K-2	34
1934	Credle, Ellis	*Down, Down the Mountain*	Nelson	3-5	39
1935	Brink, Carol R.	*Caddie Woodlawn*	Macmillan	5-7	39, 42, 91
1936	Ardizzone, Edward	*Little Tim and the Brave Sea Captain* (new ed. Walck, 1955)	Oxford (Walck)	K-2	35, 93
1936	Hunt, Mabel L.	*The Little Girl with Seven Names*	Stokes (Lippincott)	4-6	39
1936	Sawyer, Ruth	*Roller Skates*	Viking	6-8	39
1937	Geisel, Theodor (pseud. Dr. Seuss)	*And to Think That I Saw It on Mulberry Street*	Vanguard	K-3	35
1938	Daugherty, James	*Andy and the Lion*	Viking	1-3	35
1939	Haywood, Carolyn	*"B" Is for Betsy*	Harcourt	2-3	39
1940	Gates, Doris	*Blue Willow*	Viking	5-8	50
1940	McCloskey, Robert	*Lentil*	Viking	2-4	51, 93
1941	Enright, Elizabeth	*The Saturdays*	Rinehart (Holt)	4-7	51
1941	Estes, Eleanor	*The Moffats*	Harcourt	4-6	51
1942	Burton, Virginia Lee	*The Little House*	Houghton	1-4	56, 93
1943	McCloskey, Robert	*Homer Price*	Viking	4-7	51, 74, 93
1945	Lenski, Lois	*Strawberry Girl*	Lippincott	4-6	50
1948	McCloskey, Robert	*Blueberries for Sal*	Viking	K-2	56
1950	Cleary, Beverly	*Henry Huggins*	Morrow	3-6	74
1950	Milhous, Katherine	*The Egg Tree*	Scribner	1-3	68
1952	Dalgliesh, Alice	*The Bears on Hemlock Mountain*	Scribner	K-3	74
1953	Krumgold, Joseph	*. . . And Now Miguel*	Crowell	6-8	73
1955	Ets, Marie H.	*Play with Me*	Viking	K-1	69
1955	Lindquist, Jennie D.	*The Golden Name Day*	Harper	3-6	73

Date	Author	Title	Publishers	Grades	Page
1955	Sorensen, Virginia E.	*Plain Girl*	Harcourt	4-6	49, 73
1956	Udry, Janice M.	*A Tree Is Nice*	Harper	K-1	68
1958	Anglund, Joan W.	*A Friend Is Someone Who Likes You*	Harcourt	K-1	70
1958	Joslin, Sesyle	*What Do You Say, Dear?*	W. R. Scott	K-1	69
1958	Robertson, Keith	*Henry Reed, Inc.*	Viking	5-8	73, 93

CHILDREN OF OTHER LANDS

Date	Author	Title	Publishers	Grades	Page
1929	Nesbit, Edith	*The Bastable Children* (contained three books: *The Treasure Seekers, The New Treasure Seekers,* and *The Would-Be-Goods;* all three published singly, il. by Walter Hodges, Coward, 1948)	Coward (o.p.)	5-7	3
1930	Morrow, Elizabeth	*The Painted Pig* (il. by René d'Harnoncourt)	Knopf	2-4	40
1931	Lattimore, Eleanor	*Little Pear*	Harcourt	3-5	40
1931	Ransome, Arthur	*Swallows and Amazons*	Lippincott	6-9	41
1935	Aulaire, Ingri and Edgar Parin d'	*Children of the Northlights*	Viking	3-5	33
1935	Seredy, Kate	*The Good Master*	Viking	5-7	33, 41
1938	Handforth, Thomas	*Mei Li*	Doubleday	1-3	35, 67
1938	Van Stockum, Hilda	*The Cottage at Bantry Bay*	Viking	4-7	41
1939	Bemelmans, Ludwig	*Madeline*	Simon (Viking)	1-3	36
1940	Sperry, Armstrong	*Call It Courage*	Macmillan	5-8	52
1947	Treffinger, Carolyn	*Li Lun, Lad of Courage*	Abingdon	4-7	52
1948	Rankin, Louise	*Daughter of the Mountains*	Viking	5-8	52
1948	Wiese, Kurt	*Fish in the Air*	Viking	K-3	52
1950	Chönz, Selina	*A Bell for Ursli*	Oxford (Walck)	K-2	70
1951	Seignobosc, Françoise (pseud. Françoise)	*Jeanne-Marie Counts Her Sheep*	Scribner	K-1	70
1952	Clark, Ann Nolan	*Secret of the Andes*	Viking	4-7	70
1954	DeJong, Meindert	*The Wheel on the School*	Harper	4-7	6, 70
1955	Iwamatsu, Jun (pseud. Taro Yashima)	*Crow Boy*	Viking	1-3	49, 68
1955	Rugh, Belle D.	*Crystal Mountain*	Houghton	4-7	71
1955	Boston, Lucy M.	*The Children of Green Knowe*	Harcourt	4-7	75
1958	Carlson, Natalie Savage	*The Family under the Bridge*	Harper	3-5	71
1959	Ets, Marie Hall, and Labastida, Aurora	*Nine Days to Christmas*	Viking	K-3	71

ANIMAL PICTURE BOOKS AND STORIES

Date	Author	Title	Publishers	Grades	Page
1923	Falls, Charles B.	*A B C Book*	Doubleday	K-2	17
1926	James, Will	*Smoky, the Cowhorse* (new ed. 1954)	Scribner	6-9	42
1927	Mukerji, Dhan Gopal	*Gay-Neck*	Dutton	6-9	42
1931	Flack, Marjorie	*Angus and the Cat*	Doubleday	K-2	35
1933	Flack, Marjorie	*The Story about Ping*	Viking	K-3	33
1935	Stong, Phil	*Honk: the Moose*	Dodd	4-6	33
1936	Leaf, Munro	*The Story of Ferdinand*	Viking	1-4	35, 93
1938	Rawlings, Marjorie Kinnan	*The Yearling* (rev. 1946)	Scribner	7-9	43, 92

Date	Author	Title	Publishers	Grades	Page
1940	Knight, Eric	*Lassie Come-Home*	Winston (Holt)	6-9	59, 92
1941	McCloskey, Robert	*Make Way for Ducklings*	Viking	K-2	56, 93
1941	Rey, Hans A.	*Curious George*	Houghton	K-2	55
1944	Ets, Marie	*In the Forest*	Viking	K-3	57
1944	Lawson, Robert	*Rabbit Hill*	Viking	3-6	57, 93
1947	Henry, Marguerite	*Misty of Chincoteague*	Rand	5-8	59, 92
1948	Henry, Marguerite	*King of the Wind*	Rand	5-8	59
1949	Montgomery, Rutherford	*Kildee House*	Doubleday	5-7	58
1950	Geisel, Theodor (pseud. Dr. Seuss)	*If I Ran the Zoo*	Random	K-3	68
1952	Eichenberg, Fritz	*Ape in a Cape*	Harcourt	K-2	72
1952	Ward Lynd	*The Biggest Bear*	Houghton	K-3	66, 68
1953	Fischer, Hans	*Pitschi, the Kitten Who Always Wanted to Be Something Else*	Harcourt	K-3	72
1954	Fatio, Louise	*The Happy Lion*	Whittlesey	K-3	69
1956	Gipson, Frederick B.	*Old Yeller*	Harper	7-9	74
1957	Minarik, Else H.	*Little Bear*	Harper	K-2	64, 72
1957	Titus, Eve	*Anatole and the Cat*	Whittlesey	K-2	69

ADVENTURE

Date	Author	Title	Publishers	Grades	Page
1912	Masefield, John	*Jim Davis* (new ed. Macmillan, 1951)	Stokes (o.p.)	7-9	22
1923	Hawes, Charles B.	*The Dark Frigate* (new ed. 1934)	Atlantic Monthly Press (Little)	7-9	22
1925	Boyd, James	*Drums* (new ed. il. by N. C. Wyeth, 1928)	Scribner	8-9	44
1928	Kelly, Eric P.	*The Trumpeter of Krakow*	Macmillan	7-9	45
1940	Hall, Anna G.	*Nansen*	Viking	7-9	54
1942	Gray, Elizabeth Janet	*Adam of the Road*	Viking	6-9	52
1946	Jewett, Eleanore M.	*The Hidden Treasure of Glaston*	Viking	7-9	52
1947	Du Bois, William Pène	*Twenty-One Balloons*	Viking	5-9	58

AMERICANA

Date	Author	Title	Publishers	Grades	Page
1916	Meigs, Cornelia	*Master Simon's Garden* (new ed. 1929)	Macmillan	7-9	21
1926	Skinner, Constance L.	*Becky Landers, Frontier Warrior*	Macmillan	6-9	44
1928	Irving, Washington	*Knickerbocker's History of New York* (ed. by Anne C. Moore) (new ed. Ungar, 1959)	Doubleday (o.p.)	6-9	45
1928	Sandburg, Carl	*Abe Lincoln Grows Up*	Harcourt	7-9	45
1931	Armer, Laura A.	*Waterless Mountain*	Longmans	5-8	39
1932-43	Wilder, Laura I.	*Little House in the Big Woods,* and other *Little House* books (il. by Helen Sewell) (rev. ed. il. by Garth Williams, 1953) (See also separate entries.)	Harper	4-6 & 6-9 (later volumes)	42
1933	Meigs, Cornelia	*Invincible Louisa*	Little	7-9	45
1934	Coatsworth, Elizabeth	*Away Goes Sally*	Macmillan	4-6	42

Date	Author	Title	Publishers	Grades	Page
1935	Wilder, Laura I.	*Little House on the Prairie*	Harper	4-6	42
1937	Wilder, Laura I.	*On the Banks of Plum Creek*	Harper	4-6	See 42
1938	Eaton, Jeanette	*Leader by Destiny*	Harcourt	7-9	45
1939	Daugherty, James	*Daniel Boone*	Viking	5-9	45
1940	De Angeli, Marguerite	*Thee, Hannah!*	Doubleday	4-6	50
1940	Wilder, Laura I.	*The Long Winter*	Harper	5-8	49
1941	Clark, Ann Nolan	*In My Mother's House* (new ed. 1951)	Viking	2-5	50
1941	Edmonds, Walter D.	*The Matchlock Gun*	Dodd	4-6	50, 91
1943	Forbes, Esther	*Johnny Tremain*	Houghton	7-9	50
1943	Wilder, Laura I.	*These Happy Golden Years*	Harper	6-9	42, 50
1946	Forbes, Esther	*America's Paul Revere*	Houghton	5-9	54
1949	Caudill, Rebecca	*Tree of Freedom*	Viking	7-9	50, 91
1950	Judson, Clara Ingram	*Abraham Lincoln, Friend of the People*	Follett	6-9	82
1950	Yates, Elizabeth	*Amos Fortune, Free Man*	Dutton	7-9	82
1951	Commager, Henry Steele	*America's Robert E. Lee*	Houghton	6-9	81
1953	Daugherty, James	*Marcus and Narcissa Whitman, Pioneers of Oregon*	Viking	7-9	82
1953	Lawson, Robert	*Mr. Revere and I*	Little	6-8	81
1954	Dalgliesh, Alice	*The Courage of Sarah Noble*	Scribner	3-5	79
1954	Dalgliesh, Alice	*The Thanksgiving Story*	Scribner	K-3	84, 91
1955	Aulaire, Ingri and Edgar Parin d'	*Columbus*	Doubleday	3-5	81
1955	Latham, Jean Lee	*Carry On, Mr. Bowditch*	Houghton	6-9	83
1956	Dalgliesh, Alice	*Ride on the Wind*	Scribner	3-5	81
1957	Keith, Harold	*Rifles for Watie*	Crowell	7-9	80
1957	Lawson, Robert	*The Great Wheel*	Viking	7-9	80
1958	Franchere, Ruth	*Willa*	Crowell	5-7	82
1958	Speare, Elizabeth G.	*The Witch of Blackbird Pond*	Houghton	7-9	3, 21, 80
1958	Steele, William O.	*The Perilous Road*	Harcourt	5-7	80

RELIGION

Date	Author	Title	Publishers	Grades	Page
1931	Petersham, Maud and Miska (ils.)	*The Christ Child* (sel. by illustrators)	Doubleday	K-4	37
1934	Sewell, Helen (il.)	*A First Bible* (sel. and arr. by Jean West Maury from the King James Bible)	Oxford (Walck)	4-8	37
1937	Lathrop, Dorothy (il.)	*Animals of the Bible* (with text sel. by Helen Dean Fish from the King James Bible)	Stokes (Lippincott)	1-4	37
1944	Fitch, Florence	*One God; The Ways We Worship Him*	Lothrop	5-9	55

LANGUAGE

Date	Author	Title	Publishers	Grades	Page
1955	Frasconi, Antonio	*See and Say, Guarda E Parla, Mira Y Habla, Regarde et Parle*	Harcourt	3-7	76
1957	Rand, Ann and Paul	*Sparkle and Spin*	Harcourt	K-3	70
1958	Frasconi, Antonio	*The House That Jack Built; La Maison Que Jacques A Batie*	Harcourt	1-4	76

Date	Author	Title	Publishers	Grades	Page

INFORMATION: HISTORY AND GEOGRAPHY

Date	Author	Title	Publishers	Grades	Page
1911	Tappan, Eva March	*When Knights Were Bold*	Houghton	6-9	20
1921	Van Loon, Hendrik	*The Story of Mankind* (new and enlarged ed. 1951)	Boni and Liveright (Liveright)	7-9	21
1924	Hillyer, Virgil M.	*A Child's History of the World* (rev. with new material by Edward G. Huey, 1951)	Appleton	5-8	21, 44
1932	Hartman, Gertrude	*These United States and How They Came to Be* (new ed. 1935)	Macmillan	6-9	44
1941	Foster, Genevieve	*George Washington's World*	Scribner	7-9	53
1941	Holling, Holling C.	*Paddle-to-the-Sea*	Houghton	4-6	53
1941	White, Anne Terry	*Lost Worlds*	Random	6-10	53
1944	Duvoisin, Roger	*They Put Out to Sea*	Knopf	5-8	53
1948	McNeer, May Y.	*The Story of the Southwest*	Harper	4-7	53
1951	Baity, Elizabeth C.	*Americans before Columbus*	Viking	7-9	83
1953	McNeer, May Y.	*The Mexican Story*	Ariel (Farrar)	6-9	84
1958	McNeer, May Y.	*The Canadian Story*	Ariel (Farrar)	6-9	84
1958	Coy, Harold	*The Americans*	Little	7-9	83
1959	Mead, Margaret	*People and Places*	World	7-9	83
1959	Tunis, Edwin	*Indians*	World	7-9	83

INFORMATION AND PICTURE STORY BOOKS: SCIENCE AND MATHEMATICS

Date	Author	Title	Publishers	Grades	Page
1926	Liddell, Mary	*Little Machinery*	Doubleday (o. p.)	K-3	36
1930	Reed, William Maxwell	*The Earth for Sam* (rev. ed. by Paul Brandwein, 1960)	Harcourt	6-9	46
1932	Bronson, Wilfred S.	*Pollwiggle's Progress*	Macmillan	3-5	46
1933	Ditmars, Raymond	*Reptiles of the World* (first pub. 1910, Doubleday)	Macmillan	6-9	46
1934	Baker, Robert H.	*When the Stars Come Out* (rev. ed. 1954)	Viking	7-9	46
1936	Rourke, Constance	*Audubon*	Harcourt	7-9	45
1939	Burton, Virginia Lee	*Mike Mulligan and His Steam Shovel*	Houghton	1-3	36
1939	Gramatky, Hardie	*Little Toot*	Putnam	K-2	36, 93
1939	Huntington, Harriet E.	*Let's Go Outdoors*	Doubleday	1-4	47
1941	Kane, Henry B.	*The Tale of the Bullfrog*	Knopf (o.p.)	4-7	60
1944	Webber, Irma E.	*Travelers All*	W. R. Scott	2-4	60
1946	Tresselt, Alvin	*Rain Drop Splash*	Lothrop	K-1	60
1946	Zim, Herbert S.	*Elephants*	Morrow	2-4	61
1947	Tresselt, Alvin	*White Snow, Bright Snow*	Lothrop	K-1	57, 93
1947	Webb, Addison	*Birds in Their Homes*	Garden City Books	3-5	60
1948	Hader, Berta and Elmer	*The Big Snow*	Macmillan	K-3	57
1949	Zim, Herbert S.	*Homing Pigeons*	Morrow	6-9	61
1950	Billings, Henry	*Diesel-Electric 4030*	Viking	3-7	86
1950	Cormack, Maribelle M.	*The First Book of Stones*	Watts	4-6	86
1951	Schneider, Herman	*Everyday Weather and How It Works*	Whittlesey	5-8	86
1952	Parker, Bertha	*The Golden Treasury of Natural History*	Simon (Golden Press)	4-7	66

Date	Author	Title	Publishers	Grades	Page
1954	Bell, Thelma H.	*Snow*	Viking	3-7	87
1954	Fenton, Carroll Lane	*Prehistoric World*	Day	4-7	86
1954	Ravielli, Anthony	*Wonders of the Human Body*	Viking	4-8	89
1954	Rey, Hans A.	*Find the Constellations*	Houghton	4-8	85
1956	Billings, Henry	*Bridges*	Viking	7-9	89
1956	Zim, Herbert S., and Smith, Hobart M.	*Reptiles and Amphibians*	Golden Press	6-9	86
1957	Hogben, Lancelot T.	*The Wonderful World of Energy*	Garden City	7-9	66, 87
1957	Lewellen, John B.	*Understanding Electronics*	Crowell	7-8	89
1957	McCloskey, Robert	*Time of Wonder*	Viking	1-4	68
1957	Ravielli, Anthony	*An Adventure in Geometry*	Viking	7-9	89
1958	Barker, Will	*Winter-Sleeping Wildlife*	Harper	5-9	87
1958	Branley, Franklyn M.	*A Book of Satellites for You*	Crowell	1-4	85
1958	Branley, Franklyn M.	*The Nine Planets*	Crowell	6-9	88
1958	Buff, Mary and Conrad	*Elf Owl*	Viking	1-4	70
1958	Carson, Rachel	*The Sea around Us* (adap. by Anne Terry White)	Golden Press	6-9	87
1958	Cooper, Elizabeth K.	*Science in Your Own Back Yard*	Harcourt	5-8	87
1958	Gallant, Roy A.	*Exploring the Planets*	Garden City	5-9	88
1958	Meyer, Jerome S.	*Machines*	World	4-6	86

Author Index and Bibliography of Other Books

(Suggested grade placement follows publication date;
"rec. ed." designates a recommended edition.)

Bibliographies

BOOKS ABOUT CHILDREN'S BOOKS

Adams, Bess Porter	*About Books and Children*	Holt, 1953
American Institute of Graphic Arts	*The Children's Book Show*	The Institute, Periodically
American Library Association	*The Children's Library Yearbook*, No. 1	The Association (o.p.), 1929
Arbuthnot, May Hill	*Children and Books*	Scott, 1957
Barnes, Walter	*The Children's Poets*	World (Harcourt) (o.p.), 1924
Barry, Florence	*A Century of Children's Books*	Doran (Doubleday) (o.p.), 1923
Becker, May L.	*First Adventures in Reading*	Stokes (Lippincott) (o.p.), 1936
Cobb, Irvin	"A Plea for Old Cap Collier" in *Irvin Cobb at His Best*, pp. 163-195	Sun Dial Press, 1940
Darton, F. J. Harvey	*Children's Books in England: Five Centuries of Social Life*	Cambridge University Press, 1958
Duff, Annis	*Bequest of Wings; a Family's Pleasure with Books*	Viking, 1944
Eaton, Anne T.	*Reading with Children*	Viking, 1940
Eyre, Frank	*Twentieth Century Children's Books*	Longmans, 1952
Fenner, Phyllis R.	*The Proof of the Pudding: What Children Read*	Day, 1957
	Something Shared: Children and Books	Day, 1959
Hazard; Paul	*Books, Children and Men*	The Horn Book, Inc., 1960
The Horn Book, Inc.	*A Horn Book Sampler on Children's Books and Reading* (Norma R. Fryatt, ed.), Selected from 25 Years of *The Horn Book Magazine*, 1924-48	The Horn Book, Inc., 1959
Huck, Charlotte, and Young, Doris A.	*Children's Literature in the Elementary School*	Holt, 1961
James, Philip	"Children's Books of Yesterday," London, *The Studio*, Autumn Number, 1933	The Studio Publications, Inc., 1933
Jordan, Alice M.	*From Rollo to Tom Sawyer and Other Papers*	The Horn Book, Inc., 1948

Kready, Laura F.	*A Study of Fairy Tales*	Houghton, 1916
Kunitz, Stanley J., and Haycraft, Howard	*The Junior Book of Authors,* Second Edition Revised	H. W. Wilson, 1951
Mahony, Bertha E.; Latimer, Louise Payson; and Folmsbee, Beulah	*Illustrators of Children's Books, 1744-1945*	The Horn Book, Inc., 1947
Mahony, Bertha E., and Whitney, Elinor	*Five Years of Children's Books;* A Supplement to *Realms of Gold*	Doubleday, 1936
——————	*Realms of Gold in Children's Books*	Doubleday, 1929
Meigs, Cornelia, *et al.*	*A Critical History of Children's Literature*	Macmillan, 1953
Miller, Bertha M., and Field, Elinor W.	*Caldecott Medal Books: 1938-1957*	The Horn Book, Inc., 1957
——————	*Newbery Medal Books: 1922-1955*	The Horn Book, Inc., 1955
Mitchell, Lucy Sprague	*Here and Now Story Book*	Dutton, 1948
Moore, Anne Carroll	*My Roads to Childhood*	The Horn Book, Inc., 1961
——————	*The Three Owls,* Book 1 Books 2 and 3	Macmillan, 1925 Coward, 1928 & 1931
Moore, Annie E.	*Literature Old and New for Children*	Houghton, 1934
Muir, Percy	*English Children's Books, 1600-1900*	Praeger, 1954
New York Public Library	*The Contents of the Basket*	The Library, 1960
——————	*Reading without Boundaries*	The Library, 1956
Opie, Iona and Peter	*The Oxford Dictionary of Nursery Rhymes*	Oxford, 1952
Ramsey, Eloise, in collab. with Dorothy Mills Howard, American Folklore Society	*Folklore for Children and Young People*	American Folklore Society, 1952
Smith, Elva S.	*The History of Children's Literature*	American Library Association, 1937
Smith, Irene	*A History of the Newbery and Caldecott Medals*	Viking, 1957
Smith, Lillian H.	*The Unreluctant Years*	American Library Association, 1953
Targ, William (ed.)	*Bibliophile in the Nursery, a Bookman's Treasury of Collectors' Lore on Old and Rare Children's Books*	World, 1957
Viguers, Ruth Hill; Dalphin, Marcia; and Miller, Bertha Mahony	*Illustrators of Children's Books, 1946-56*	The Horn Book, Inc., 1958

| White, Dorothy Neal | *About Books for Children* | Oxford University Press, 1946 |
| White, Gleason | "Children's Books and Their Illustrators," London, *The Studio,* Winter Number, 1898 | The Studio Publications, Inc., 1898 |

PERIODICALS DEALING WITH CHILDREN'S BOOKS

American Library Association	*Book List*	50 E. Huron St., Chicago 11, Ill.
Center for Children's Books	*Bulletin of the Center for Children's Books*	Graduate Library School, University of Chicago, Chicago 37, Ill.
The Horn Book, Inc.	*The Horn Book Magazine*	585 Boylston St., Boston 16, Mass.
National Congress of Parents and Teachers	*The PTA Magazine*	700 N. Rush St., Chicago 11, Ill.
National Council of Teachers of English	*Elementary English*	508 S. Sixth St., Champaign, Ill.
New York Herald Tribune	*Books*	230 W. 41st St., New York 36, N. Y.
R. R. Bowker Company	*Library Journal*	1180 Avenue of the Americas, New York, N. Y.
Stines House	*The Junior Bookshelf*	Kirkburton, Huddersfield, England

HELPFUL LISTS OF CHILDREN'S BOOKS

American Association for the Advancement of Science	*The Travelling Elementary School Science Library Book List*	The Association, Annually
American Association for the Advancement of Science and the National Science Foundation	*The Science Book List for Children* (Hilary J. Deason, comp.)	The Association, 1960
Association for Childhood Education International —Literature Committee	*A Bibliography of Books for Children*	The Association, 1961
————————————	*Children's Books for $1.25 or Less*	The Association, 1959
American Library Association	*A Basic Book Collection for Elementary Grades*	The Association, 1960
————————————	*A Basic Book Collection for Junior High Schools*	The Association, 1960

Arbuthnot, May Hill, *et al.*	*Children's Books Too Good to Miss*	The Press of Western Reserve University, 1963
Baker, Augusta	*Books about Negro Life for Children*	New York Public Library, 1961
————————	*Stories; A List of Stories to Tell and to Read Aloud*	New York Public Library, 1958
Child Study Association of America	*The Children's Bookshelf; A Parents' Guide to Good Books for Boys and Girls*	Bantam Books, 1962
Compton's Pictured Encyclopedia	*Seven Stories High* (Anne Carroll Moore, *et al.*, comp.)	F. E. Compton, 1961
Crosby, Muriel (ed.)	*Reading Ladders for Human Relations*	American Council on Education, 1963
Eakin, Mary K.	*Good Books for Children; A Selection of Outstanding Children's Books Published 1948-1957*	University of Chicago Press, 1959
Eaton, Anne Thaxter	*Treasure for the Taking*	Viking, 1957
Enoch Pratt Free Library, Baltimore	*Stories to Tell; a List of Stories with Annotations*	The Library, 1956
Frank, Josette	*Your Child's Reading Today*	Doubleday, 1960
Guilfoile, Elizabeth	*Books for Beginning Readers*	National Council of Teachers of English, 1962
Heller, Frieda M.	"I Can Read It Myself," Bulletin No. 1, *Study of Independent Reading*	Center for School Experimentation, College of Education, Ohio State University, 1960
Huus, Helen	*Children's Books to Enrich the Social Studies for the Elementary Grades,* Bulletin No. 32	National Council for the Social Studies, 1961
Larrick, Nancy	*A Parent's Guide to Children's Reading* (also in Pocket Books)	Doubleday, 1958
————————	*A Teacher's Guide to Children's Books*	Merrill, 1960
Library Journal	*Best Books for Children*	R. R. Bowker, Annually
Lines, Kathleen M. (comp.)	*Four to Fourteen*	Cambridge University Press, 1950
National Congress of Parents and Teachers and the Children's Services Division of the American Library Association	*Let's Read Together; Books for Family Enjoyment*	American Library Association, 1960

National Council of Teachers of English	*Adventuring with Books;* A List for Elementary Schools (with Supplements)	The Council, 1960
	Your Reading; A List for Junior High Schools (with Supplements)	The Council, 1960
———————————		
Thomson, Jean (ed.)	*Books for Boys and Girls*	Ryerson Press, 1954
World Book Encyclopedia	*Literature for Children*	Field Enterprises, Inc., 1961

LISTINGS OF BOOKS OF THE YEAR

American Library Association, Children's Services Division	*Notable Children's Books of* ——	50 E. Huron St., Chicago 11, Ill.
Child Study Association of America, Inc.	*Books of the Year for Children*	9 E. 89th St., New York 28, N. Y.
Independent Schools Education Board	*Current Books: Junior Booklist* (Annually)	Milton 86, Mass.
Library Journal	*Recommended Children's Books* (E. Louise Davis, comp.)	1180 Avenue of the Americas, New York, N. Y.
New York Public Library	*Children's Books Suggested as Holiday Gifts*	Fifth Ave. and 42nd St., New York 18, N. Y.
The PTA Magazine	*Notable Books of* ——	700 N. Rush St., Chicago 11, Ill.
Publishers' Weekly	*Fall Children's Book Number* (in July)	1180 Avenue of the Americas, New York, N. Y.
	Spring Children's Book Number (in February)	

See also the annual Children's Book Week Sunday editions (November) of such newspapers as the *New York Herald Tribune,* the *New York Times,* the *Chicago Tribune,* and the *Washington Post;* also the Book Week number of *Saturday Review* magazine.

BIBLIOGRAPHICAL SOURCES FOR OLD BOOKS

Blanck, Jacob	*Peter Parley to Penrod*	R. R. Bowker, 1956
Pierpont Morgan Library	*Children's Literature, Books and Manuscripts:* An Exhibition, November 19, 1954, through February 28, 1955	The Library, 1954
Rosenbach, Abraham S. Wolf	*Early American Children's Books*	Southworth, 1933
Toronto Public Library	*The Osborne Collection of Early Children's Books, 1566-1910*	The Library, 1958

REFERENCE SOURCES

American Library Association	*Subject and Title Index to Short Stories for Children*	The Association, 1955
Brewton, John E.	*Index to Children's Poetry*	H. W. Wilson, 1942
————————————	*Index to Children's Poetry* (First Supplement)	H. W. Wilson, 1954
Eakin, Mary K.	*Subject Index to Books for Primary Grades*	American Library Association, 1961
Rue, Eloise	*Subject Index to Books for Intermediate Grades*	American Library Association, 1950
H. W. Wilson Company	*Children's Catalog* (with Supplements 1909–date)	H. W. Wilson, 1961

Directory of Current Publishing Companies

ABINGDON. Abingdon Press, 201 Eighth Ave. S., Nashville 3, Tenn.

APPLETON. Appleton-Century-Crofts, 34 W. 33 St., New York 1, N. Y.

BARNES. A. S. Barnes. See Yoseloff.

BOBBS. The Bobbs-Merrill Co., Inc., 4300 W. 62 St., Indianapolis 6, Ind.

BRITISH BOOK CENTRE. British Book Centre, Inc., 122 E. 55 St., New York 22, N. Y.

CHILDRENS PRESS. Childrens Press, Inc., Jackson Blvd. & Racine Ave., Chicago 7, Ill.

COWARD. Coward-McCann, Inc., 200 Madison Ave., New York 16, N. Y.

CROWELL. Thomas Y. Crowell, 201 Park Ave. S., New York 3, N. Y.

DAY. The John Day Co., Inc., 62 W. 45 St., New York 36, N. Y.

DODD. Dodd, Mead & Co., 432 Park Ave. S., New York 16, N. Y.

DOUBLEDAY. Doubleday & Co., Inc., Garden City, N. Y.

DUTTON. E. P. Dutton & Co., Inc., 201 Park Ave. S., New York 3, N. Y.

FARRAR. Farrar, Straus & Cudahy, Inc., 19 Union Square W., New York 3, N. Y.

FOLLETT. Follett Publishing Co., 1010 W. Washington Blvd., Chicago 7, Ill.

GARDEN CITY BOOKS. See Doubleday.

GINN. Ginn & Co., Statler Bldg., Back Bay P. O. 191, Boston 17, Mass.

GOLDEN PRESS. Golden Press, Inc., 850 Third Ave., New York 22, N. Y.

GROSSET. Grosset & Dunlap, Inc., 1107 Broadway, New York 10, N. Y.

HALE. E. M. Hale & Co., 1201 S. Hastings Way, Eau Claire, Wis.

HARCOURT. Harcourt, Brace & World, Inc., 750 Third Ave., New York 17, N. Y.

HARPER. Harper & Row, Publishers, 49 E. 33 St., New York 16, N. Y.

HEATH. D. C. Heath & Co., 285 Columbus Ave., Boston 16, Mass.

HOLIDAY. Holiday House, 8 W. 13 St., New York 11, N. Y.

HOLT. Holt, Rinehart & Winston, Inc., 383 Madison Ave., New York 17, N. Y.

HORN BOOK. The Horn Book, Inc., 585 Boylston St., Boston 16, Mass.

HOUGHTON. Houghton Mifflin Co., 2 Park St., Boston 7, Mass.

KNOPF. Alfred A. Knopf, Inc., 501 Madison Ave., New York 22, N. Y.

LIPPINCOTT. J. B. Lippincott Co., E. Washington Square, Philadelphia 5, Pa.

LITTLE. Little, Brown & Co., 34 Beacon St., Boston 6, Mass.

LIVERIGHT. Liveright Publishing Corp., 386 Park Ave. S., New York 16, N. Y.

LONGMANS. See David McKay.

LOTHROP. Lothrop, Lee & Shepard Co., Inc., 419 Park Ave. S., New York 16, N. Y.

MACMILLAN. The Macmillan Co., 60 Fifth Ave., New York 11, N. Y.

McGRAW-HILL. McGraw-Hill Book Co., Inc., 330 W. 42 St., New York 36, N. Y.

McKAY. David McKay Co., Inc., 119 W. 40 St., New York 18, N. Y.

MESSNER. Julian Messner, Inc., 8 W. 40 St., New York 18, N. Y.

MORROW. William Morrow & Co., Inc., 425 Park Ave. S., New York 16, N. Y.

NELSON. Thomas Nelson & Sons, 18 E. 41 St., New York 17, N. Y.
OXFORD. Oxford University Press, Inc., 417 Fifth Ave., New York 16, N. Y.
PANTHEON. Pantheon Books, Inc., 22 E. 51 St., New York 22, N. Y.
PRENTICE-HALL. Prentice-Hall, Inc., Englewood Cliffs, N. J.
PUTNAM. G. P. Putnam's Sons, 200 Madison Ave., New York 16, N. Y.
RAND. Rand McNally & Co., 8255 Central Park Ave., Skokie, Ill.
RANDOM. Random House, Inc., 457 Madison Ave., New York 22, N. Y.
RUSSELL. Russell & Russell, Inc., 80 E. 11 St., New York 3, N. Y.
SCOTT. Scott, Foresman & Co., 433 Erie St., Chicago 11, Ill.
W. R. SCOTT. William R. Scott, Inc., 8 W. 13 St., New York 11, N. Y.
SCRIBNER. Charles Scribner's Sons, 597 Fifth Avenue, New York 17, N. Y.
UNGAR. Frederick Ungar Publishing Co., Inc., 131 E. 23 St., New York 10, N. Y.
VANGUARD. Vanguard Press, 424 Madison Ave., New York 17, N. Y.
VIKING. The Viking Press, Inc., 625 Madison Ave., New York 22, N. Y.
WALCK. Henry Z. Walck, Inc. 101 Fifth Ave., New York 3, N. Y.
WARNE. Frederick Warne & Co., Inc., 210 Fifth Ave., New York 10, N. Y.
WATTS. Franklin Watts, Inc., 575 Lexington Ave., New York 22, N. Y.
WESTMINSTER PRESS. The Westminster Press, Witherspoon Bldg., Philadelphia 7, Pa.
WHITMAN. Whitman Publishing Co., 1220 Mound Ave., Racine, Wis.
WHITTLESEY. See McGraw-Hill.
WORLD. The World Publishing Co., 2231 W. 110 St., Cleveland 2, Ohio
YOSELOFF. Thomas Yoseloff, Publisher, 11 E. 36 St., New York 36, N. Y.
YOUNG SCOTT BOOKS. See W. R. Scott.

Index of Titles

T

U

V

W

General Index

Historical writing
Factual, 7-8, 9, 21, 44, 53, 64, 83-85, 91
Fictional, 7-9, 20, 21-22, 44-45, 52, 79-80
Home Reading, 25
Horn Book, Incorporated, The, 23
Horn Book Magazine, The, 27, 28, 65
Hosic, James F., 26
Humor, 35, 78-79, 93
Huey, Edward G., 21
Hunt, Clara W., 28

I

Imaginative stories, 11, 17, 38-39, 57-58, 74-78, 92
"Immortal Four," 5
Independent reading, 24, 28, 63
Individualized reading, 63, 93
International Geophysical Year, 89
International Kindergarten Union, 47
International understanding, 28, 40, 48-49, 70-73
See also Children around the world.
International Youth Book Exhibit, 49

J

Jordan, Alice M., 2
Junior Literary Guild, 47, 67

L

Laura Ingalls Wilder Award, 42, 82
Lawson, Robert, 39, 40, 54, 81
Lesser, Margaret, 49
Library Journal, 65
Library Service Division (USOE), 47
Library standards, 24, 25, 28, 66
Lindquist, Jennie, 27, 73
Lofting, Hugh, 17, 28
Longmans, 13

M

Mabie, Hamilton Wright, 31
Mackintosh, Helen, 28
Macmillan Company, 24, 27
Mahony, Bertha. See Miller, Bertha Mahony.

Manhasset, New York, Schools, 48, 77
Mass communication, 49, 62, 92
Massee, May, 24, 33
Mathiews, Franklin K., 5, 26
Meigs, Cornelia, 42
Melcher, Frederic G., 6, 22, 26, 27, 37, 48
Metropolitan Museum of Art, 62
Junior Museum, 62
Meyer, Jerome S., 61, 86
"Mile-a-minute" books, 5
Miller, Bertha Mahony, 27
Mitchell, Lucy Sprague, 29
Moore, Anne Carroll, 23, 24, 29, 33, 45
Moral tales, 1-3
Moral Tales, 2
Morley, Christopher, 36
Motion pictures, 22
My Roads to Childhood, 23
Music. See Fine arts.

N

National Association of School Librarians, 25
National Children's Book Week, 6, 26, 28, 49
National Committee on the Reorganization of English in the Secondary Schools, 26
National Council of Teachers of English, 1, 12, 25, 26, 27, 28, 48, 65
National Defense Education Act, 63
National Education Association, 24, 25, 48
National parks, 22
Nature books, 46-47, 57, 60-61, 66
Nature stories, 9-11, 58, 68, 70
New York Herald Tribune: Books, 23
New York Public Library, 23
Newbery Award, 21, 24, 27, 33, 39, 42, 45, 50, 73
Newbery Medal Books: 1922-1925, 27
Nicholson, William, 17, 34
"Noble" boys, 3
Notable Children's Books of the Year, 65

O

Oversized books, 66
Overstreet, Harry, 30
Office of the German Military Government, 49
Offset printing, 33

Typography:

    *Type faces selected for this publication are Caledonia, Futura
Medium, Ronaldson, Spartan Book Heavy and Tempo Bold.*